The Sustainable Development Goals in International Law and Policy

This book introduces the reader to the Sustainable Development Goals (SDGs) in an accessible and concise way, examining sustainable development from an international law and policy perspective.

The SDGs seek to stimulate social, economic and environmental action to achieve peace and prosperity for all people and the planet. The book examines the SDGs in an approachable and engaging way, situating the goals in the broader context of international law and policy efforts to achieve sustainable development. Beginning by exploring the background to the SDGs, the book includes the historical, politico-legal and developmental context, their broad scope, and how they are enabled, measured and tracked. It then discusses the SDGs thematically, explaining how they are underpinned by and contribute to international law and policy, as well as exploring the interlinkages between the goals and targets. Finishing with a future-focused perspective, the book suggests opportunities and initiatives which can advance the SDGs.

The book will be of interest to researchers and practitioners in the field of international law, environmental studies and sustainable development.

Erika Techera is a professor of law at the University of Western Australia. Her research focuses on international and comparative environmental law. She is a former barrister and fellow of the Australian Academy of Law.

Routledge Research in International Law

Rural and Remote Communities as Non-State Actors
A Legal and Moral Argument
Ciprian Nicolae Radavoi and David Price

Public Interest Litigation in International Law
Justine Bendel and Yusra Suedi

Law Reforms around the World
An International Economic Law Perspective
Edited by Asif H. Qureshi

Towards an Independent Kurdistan
Self-Determination in International Law
Loqman Radpey

The African Continental Free Trade Area Agreement
Legal and Policy Frameworks
Collins C. Ajibo

Theory of Obligations in International Law
Cezary Mik

International Investment Law Reform
Contemporary Issues and Solutions
Edited by Obiajunwa Ama

The Sustainable Development Goals in International Law and Policy
Erika Techera

For more information about this series, please visit www.routledge.com/Routledge-Research-in-International-Law/book-series/INTNLLAW

The Sustainable Development Goals in International Law and Policy

Erika Techera

Routledge
Taylor & Francis Group
LONDON AND NEW YORK

First published 2025
by Routledge
4 Park Square, Milton Park, Abingdon, Oxon OX14 4RN

and by Routledge
605 Third Avenue, New York, NY 10158

Routledge is an imprint of the Taylor & Francis Group, an informa business

British Library Cataloguing-in-Publication Data
A catalogue record for this book is available from the British Library

ISBN: 978-1-032-94913-0 (hbk)
ISBN: 978-1-032-95262-8 (pbk)
ISBN: 978-1-003-58398-1 (ebk)

DOI: 10.4324/9781003583981

Typeset in Times New Roman
by Apex CoVantage, LLC

Contents

Preface

The Sustainable Development Goals (SDGs) are a unique product of their time. Adopted in 2015 with the aim of being achieved by 2030, the SDGs seek to drive the transformative changes needed to reshape our world and ensure sustainable futures. They build on the earlier Millennium Development Goals and complement the objectives of many international institutions and legal instruments. The SDGs cover a diversity of global social, developmental and environmental challenges. Although the 17 goals are individual, they are inherently interconnected, and they must all be achieved to secure sustainable futures for all people and the planet that we rely so heavily upon.

The SDGs are so critical that everyone should be able to understand and contribute to them. Yet often international initiatives such as this are opaque, poorly explained and not contextualised for non-expert audiences. This book was driven by the need for a resource for university students that examined the SDGs in an accessible and straightforward way. Yet this book is intended for all educated audiences, from any discipline and of any age, interested in engaging with the vital goals. This book responds to these needs for an advanced introduction to the SDGs that explains their origins and linkages to other United Nations developments, as well as exploring them in some detail.

I would like to thank my wonderful colleagues who reviewed chapters of the book and provided vital feedback that helped to improve it in myriad ways. This collegial support is one of the benefits of working in an academic institution. In particular, I owe thanks to Sharon Mascher, Fiona McGaughey, Aidan Ricciardo, Renae Barker, Alvin Yap, John Chandler and Joe Clare. I also thank Routledge, who agreed to publish this volume and to do so in a truncated time frame to enable readers to have access to it in a timely way. I would also like to acknowledge the independent reviewers of the proposal for this book who supported its publication.

The book indicates the perspectives of the author. The content of this publication has not been approved by the United Nations and does not reflect the views of the United Nations or its officials or Member States. The United Nations Sustainable Development Goals web site can be accessed at https://www.un.org/sustainabledevelopment/.

Abbreviations

CBD	Convention on Biological Diversity
CFCs	Chlorofluorocarbons
CRC	Convention on the Rights of the Child
FAO	Food and Agriculture Organisation
GBF	Kunming-Montreal Global Biodiversity Framework
HLPF	UN High-Level Political Forum on Sustainable Development
ICCPR	International Covenant on Civil and Political Rights
ICERD	International Convention on the Elimination of All Forms of Racial Discrimination
ICESCR	International Covenant on Economic, Social and Cultural Rights
ILO	International Labour Organisation
IMF	International Monetary Fund
IOC	Intergovernmental Oceanographic Commission
IP	Intellectual property
MARPOL	International Convention for the Prevention of Pollution from Ships
MDGs	Millennium Development Goals
SDGs	Sustainable Development Goals
SIDS	Small Island Developing States
TRIPS	Agreement on Trade-Related Aspects of Intellectual Property Rights
UDHR	Universal Declaration on Human Rights
UN	United Nations
UNCTAD	UN Conference on Trade and Development
UNDP	UN Development Program
UNDRR	UN Office for Disaster Risk Reduction
UNEP	UN Environment Program
UNESCO	UN Educational, Scientific and Cultural Organization
UNFCCC	UN Framework Convention on Climate Change
UNGA	UN General Assembly
WB	World Bank

WHO	World Health Organisation
WIPO	World Intellectual Property Organization
WTO	World Trade Organization

Glossary

Accession is a formal step in international law-making. Once a nation has acceded to a treaty, for example, it is legally bound by it in a similar way to signature and ratification.

Access to justice involves awareness and exercise of legal rights (such as challenging discrimination or holding decision makers accountable), the provision of legal aid services and rights of standing before courts and tribunals.

Adoption of an international instrument (e.g., a treaty or a declaration) is the process by which nations agree to the document and the wording within it. This usually occurs through the United Nations resolutions.

Anthropocentric means human-centred and is used to explain thinking and approaches which prioritise humans over other living and non-living things.

Compliance is a step before enforcement when those bound by the law voluntarily abide by it. Where they do not, authorities can impose non-compliance measures which if unsuccessful may lead to formal enforcement.

Convention is used interchangeably with treaty or international agreement to mean a legally binding document adopted by nations by consensus.

Declaration means a non-binding international document or instrument adopted by consensus, usually through the United Nations.

Dualist system means that for an international law treaty to apply to people and corporations within a nation, after the treaty is ratified the rules and obligations must be incorporated into domestic legislation (i.e., acts or statutes).

Enforcement is the process of holding a nation (or person or corporation) to account if it breaches or breaks legal rules.

Governance has no universal definition but can be described as the way in which societies, governments and organisations are managed and led. Good governance is best described as a set of principles that includes accountability, transparency, efficiency, effectiveness, inclusivity, equity and the rule of law.

Indicators are aligned with specific targets under each SDG and detail the data used to measure progress on the target.

Instrument is used in this book to mean a document adopted by nations, usually through the United Nations. An international instrument can be legally binding (e.g., a treaty or convention) or non-binding (e.g., a declaration).

Legally binding means that an instrument, or obligation within it, can be enforced if breached.

Legislation is formal, legally binding (enforceable), written law. It can take the form of statutes and acts, although other words can be used to describe these documents, such as ordinances, decrees, regulations and codes.

Millennium Development Goals (MDGs) were eight goals adopted by the international community during the Millennium Summit in 2000. They were a precursor to the SDGs.

Monist systems are those in which international law applies directly to citizens and corporations within a nation as soon as that country ratifies the treaty or convention.

Preamble is the preliminary section of an international instrument and is explanatory but not legally binding.

Ratification is a formal step in international law-making. It occurs after the treaty or other international instrument is signed by a representative of a state. Most nations include in their constitutions, for example, the requirement that the government representative must table the treaty before parliament, which must then ratify (agree or endorse the signing of the treaty) that the nation should be bound by the obligations.

Rule of law at its simplest means that everyone (citizens, corporations and governments) is equally bound by the same laws and entitled to equal protections under the law.

Signature is how nations begin the process of being bound by an international instrument. A government representative can sign a treaty during the period that it is open for signature.

Soft law is used to mean non-legally binding obligations, often set out in informal law instruments such as UN Declarations. Soft law instruments are not intended to be enforceable but rather to stimulate action.

Sovereignty relates to supreme authority, meaning autonomy of a state or within it.

States is used interchangeably with nations to mean countries recognised by the United Nations.

Sustainable development was defined in 1987 as development that 'meets the needs of the present without compromising the ability of future generations to meet their own needs'. It is explained as three pillars which balance economic, social and environmental concerns.

Sustainable Development Goals (SDGs) are the 17 principal goals set out in Agenda 2030 which seek to drive the changes needed for sustainable development.

Target in terms of the SDGs, a specific aim under a main SDG which may be numbered or lettered depending on whether it focuses on a substantive or implementation measure.

Treaty is used interchangeably with convention or international agreement to mean a legally binding international law instrument adopted by nations by consensus.

Timeline of international conferences, events and treaties

Soft Initiatives	*Date*	*Legally Binding Agreements*
Food and Agriculture Organization created	**1945**	UN Charter
World Health Organization created Universal Declaration on Human Rights	**1948**	
UN Conference on Trade and Development (UNCTAD) established	**1964**	
	1965	Convention on the Elimination of All Forms of Racial Discrimination
	1966	International Covenant on Civil and Political Rights International Covenant on Economic, Social and Cultural Rights
UN Conference on the Human Environment (known as the 'Stockholm Conference') Stockholm Declaration UN Environment Program (UNEP) is created	**1972**	
	1979	Convention on the Elimination of All Forms of Discrimination Against Women
Our Common Future ('Brundtland Report')	**1987**	
	1989	ILO Indigenous and Tribal Peoples Convention UN Convention on the Rights of the Child

(*Continued*)

(Continued)

Soft Initiatives	*Date*	*Legally Binding Agreements*
	1990	International Convention on the Protection of the Rights of All Migrant Workers and Members of Their Families
UN Conference on Environment and Development (the 'Rio Conference') Rio Declaration and Agenda 21 UN Commission on Sustainable Development	**1992**	Convention on Biological Diversity UN Framework Convention on Climate Change
World Food Summit and Action Plan	**1996**	Rome Declaration on World Food Security
	1997	Decade for The Eradication for Poverty
UN Global Compact	**1999**	
Millennium Summit UN Millennium Declaration	**2000**	
World Summit for Sustainable Development	**2002**	
	2006	Convention on the Rights of Persons with Disabilities
Declaration on the Rights of Indigenous Peoples	**2007**	
2nd UN Decade for the Eradication of Poverty	**2008**	
Summit on the MDGs	**2010**	
UN Decade on Biodiversity	**2011**	
UN Conference on Sustainable Development	**2012**	
Agenda 2030 and the SDGs adopted	**2015**	Paris Agreement
UN Decade of Action on Nutrition	**2016**	
3rd UN Decade for Eradication of Poverty International Decade for Action "Water for Sustainable Development" Adoption of Indicators to support SDGs	**2018**	
UN Declaration on universal health coverage	**2019**	
Decade of Action to deliver the SDGs	**2020**	
UN Decade on Ecosystem Restoration UN Decade of Ocean Science for Sustainable Development	**2021**	
International Decade of Sciences for Sustainable Development	**2024**	

1 Introduction to the Sustainable Development Goals

1.1 Overview

Societal issues have been at the core of the United Nations (UN) since its formation in 1945, in the shadow of World War II. The *UN Charter* (1945) demonstrates this with reference to 'tolerance', 'peace and security', 'faith in fundamental human rights' and 'social progress and better standards of life' (Preamble).[1] The *UN Charter* also mentions 'justice and respect for the obligations arising from treaties' immediately connecting it with international law. Later in the 20th century, environmental concerns emerged, as did growing awareness of the link between human rights and environment. Initial attention focused on pollution and endangered species, but it has since become clear that we face unprecedented pressures that have led to a triple planetary crisis.[2] Unsustainable consumption and production, over-exploitation of natural resources, dependency upon fossil fuels, and the pursuit of limitless growth are the causes of these problems.[3] Simultaneously, may socio-cultural challenges such as poverty, food insecurity and inequality remain unresolved and compromise the achievement of environmental outcomes. The solution, it is argued, lies in achieving sustainable development, a concept which emerged in the 1980s to balance human needs, both economic and social, with the needs of the natural environment. Since then, sustainable development has become a 'global priority [and] a principle of international law' and has led to 'a universal framework known as the Sustainable Development Goals'.[4]

The Sustainable Development Goals (SDGs) are both an international pledge and a call to action.[5] They are relevant for all nations, both developed

1 UN Charter, https://www.un.org/en/about-us/un-charter.
2 UN Climate Change, 'What is the Triple Planetary Crisis?' *UNFCCC Blog*, Apr 13, 2022, https://unfccc.int/news/what-is-the-triple-planetary-crisis.
3 Niamh Guiry, 'International Law & the Sustainable Development Goals' (2024) 7 *The Boolean* 1.
4 Guiry (2024) 2.
5 A critical resource is the official UN SDGs homepage: https://www.un.org/sustainabledevelopment and https://sdgs.un.org/goals.

DOI: 10.4324/9781003583981-1

and developing countries. The SDGs are contained in *Transforming Our World: Agenda 2030 for Sustainable Development*, which was unanimously endorsed by UN member states in 2015 at the United Nations Summit on Sustainable Development.[6] The vision is ambitious, with the objective of ensuring that 'no one will be left behind' (Preamble). *Agenda 2030* seeks to provide 'a plan of action for people, planet and prosperity' and included within it 'a comprehensive, far-reaching and people-centred set of universal and transformative Goals and targets' (para 2). The 17 goals and 169 targets are separate and yet also 'integrated and indivisible and balance the three dimensions of sustainable development: the economic, social and environmental' (Preamble).[7] The progress of the SDGs is monitored and assessed using 232 indicators.

The SDGs are said to be a 'unique product of their time'.[8] They can be understood as a major development because they continue the fight against ongoing challenges – such as poverty, hunger, health and inequality – but add the imperative of advancing the equitable distribution of Earth's limited resources. The SDGs are also unique for the involvement of civil society in their development, their widespread global endorsement and subsequent implementation through myriad actions at scales from the global to the local.

There is little doubt that achieving the SDGs will require input from multiple disciplines. A range of social sciences (law, politics and international relations, public policy and administration) are all critical to the global architecture under which the SDGs sit, and other fields (economics, business and finance) will be needed to achieve the goals. Other areas will also be vital including health sciences (medicine, global and population health), natural sciences (agricultural and environmental management, etc.), engineering (energy production and infrastructure, etc.) and technological sciences (information technology, computer and data science).

This book explores the SDGs through a legal lens, in part, because the goals are said to be 'rooted explicitly in the law and policy of sustainable development'.[9] By examining the SDGs from a legal perspective it is possible to understand how international law informs the goals and targets and can

6 This document was adopted by the United Nations General Assembly Resolution by all 193 member states of the UN: see United Nations, *Transforming Our World: The 2030 Agenda for Sustainable Development* (*Agenda 2030*) (2015), https://sdgs.un.org/2030agenda.

7 *Agenda 2030,* Preamble.

8 Ilias Bantekas and Katerina Akestoridi, 'Sustainable Development Goals, between Politics and Soft Law: The Emergence of "Political Normativity" in International Law' (2023) 37 *Emory International Law Review* 499, 504.

9 Dire Tladi, 'SDG1: End Poverty in All Its Forms Everywhere' in J Ebbesson and E Hey (eds), *The Cambridge Handbook of The Sustainable Development Goals and International Law* (Cambridge: Cambridge University Press, 2022) 55.

support their achievement, as well as how the SDGs contribute to international law and its objectives.

This chapter provides the context and background to the SDGs and their place in the evolution of sustainable development law and policy more broadly. Chapters 2–8 explore each of the SDGs in detail. Although all of the goals are interrelated and must be achieved collectively, they have been separated into clusters in these chapters aligned with social, economic and environmental elements. Chapter 9 examines how progress is measured, as well as the actions needed now and in the coming years to advance the goals to meet the 2030 targets.

1.2 International law and its relevance

International law is the body of laws agreed to by nations (states) and developed and adopted by consensus. It includes rules, norms and standards, as well as rights and obligations, contained in instruments such as treaties, conventions and international agreements. International law includes treaties or conventions which are global agreements drafted and adopted by member states through the UN.[10] Once a state becomes a party to a treaty it is bound by the obligations set out in that instrument. Although there is no global enforcement body, other nations may bring proceedings through global courts such as the International Court of Justice.[11]

In contrast, international 'soft law' (also known as 'informal law') is aspirational only and contains voluntary commitments that cannot be legally enforced. Examples include the *Universal Declaration on Human Rights* and the *Declaration on the Rights of Indigenous Peoples*. Although not binding on nations, soft law can be highly influential in shaping behaviour and actions.

The SDGs are soft law and not legally enforceable. They are contained in *Agenda 2030*, adopted by a UN General Assembly (UNGA) Resolution, and such resolutions are never legally binding. Yet it is clear from their wording that they build upon international law and were 'intended to have normative effect . . . to influence and change the behaviour of states and other stakeholders'.[12] Furthermore, some of the SDGs name international conventions and

10 For example, the *UN Framework Convention on Climate Change* and the *Paris Agreement*.

11 Many countries, such as Australia, New Zealand, Canada, the UK and India, have a dualist system in which international law does not apply directly; it must be implemented through domestic legislation. Some countries, however, are monist, and international law applies automatically – such as Belgium, France, Germany, Japan and the majority of Latin American nations.

12 Karen Scott, 'SDG 14: Conserve and Sustainably Use the Oceans, Seas and Marine Resources for Sustainable Development' in J Ebbesson and E Hey (eds), *The Cambridge Handbook of The Sustainable Development Goals and International Law* (Cambridge: Cambridge University Press, 2022) 354–375, 363.

documents produced by key global organisations. Lastly, the SDGs play a role in filling some gaps in international law by adding future-focused targets and indicators and by linking together diverse legal fields.

1.3 History and evolution of the SDGs

The evolution of sustainable development, leading to the SDGs, can be seen across various conferences, agreements and outcome documents from 1945 through to 2015. A timeline of key events is included at the start of this chapter, and these developments are explored in the following sections.

1.3.1 Sustainable development in international law

The SDGs have their origin in global conferences and summits which began shortly after the formation of the UN in 1945. This series of conferences drew out the interconnectedness of people and planet: 'how the relationship between human beings and their natural environment is an essential element of the global system within which development is pursued'.[13] Relevantly, the *UN Charter* includes a duty for nations to cooperate to achieve human rights and fundamental freedoms (Articles 1, 55 and 56), and ultimately the SDGs are an example of such cooperation. As early as 1949 the UN hosted a scientific conference on conservation and use of resources, but, it was not until the UN Conference on the Human Environment (1972) (also known as the Stockholm Conference) that the global community first considered emerging environmental degradation in the context of rapid industrialisation and economic development.[14] One outcome of that conference was the *Stockholm Declaration*, which sets out 26 foundational principles to guide environmental law and decision-making.[15] At that time, sustainability and sustainable development were not referred to at all, although several principles imply the need to conduct human activities in ways that protect the natural environment both now and for the future. For example, Principle 1 included the 'fundamental right to freedom, equality and adequate conditions of life, in an environment of quality that permits a life of dignity and well-being', and Principle 2 that the 'natural resources of the earth . . . must be safeguarded for the benefit of present and future generations'. Furthermore, it was noted that the 'capacity of the earth to produce vital renewable resources

13 Bantekas and Akestoridi (2023) 537.

14 United Nations, *United Nations Conference on the Human Environment*, https://www.un.org/en/conferences/environment/stockholm1972.

15 United Nations, *Report of the United Nations Conference on the Human Environment* (A/Res/2994, December 15, 1972).

must be maintained' (Principle 4) and that 'non-renewable resources . . . must be employed in such a way as to guard against the danger of their future exhaustion' (Principle 5). The *Stockholm Declaration* was not limited to environmental matters, however, and Principle 8 raised broader concerns by stating that 'economic and social development is essential for ensuring a favorable living and working environment . . . and for creating conditions on earth that are necessary for the improvement of the quality of life'. In addition, Principles 10 and 12 highlighted the particular needs of developing countries, Principles 13–15 focused on development planning and management, and other Principles addressed demographic policies, national institutions and science and technology.

In 1986 the UNGA first recognised the right to development as a human right.[16] Yet the phrase 'sustainable development' did not appear until 1987 when the World Commission on Environment and Development (Brundtland Commission) published the report *Our Common Future*.[17] The Commission addressed development in the context of global differences in the extent of economic growth and the distribution of costs and benefits, recognising the need for greater equity across the globe (intragenerational equity) as well as for future generations (inter-generational equity). *Our Common Future* contained the words that define sustainable development: development 'that meets the needs of the present without compromising the ability of future generations to meet their own needs' (para 27). Sustainable development has been conceived of as three mutually reinforcing pillars of economic, social and environmental concerns all of which are needed to achieve sustainability. Although articulated as separate elements, it is their integration which lies at the heart of sustainable development – finding ways to balance the components is the key.

The next global environmental conference was the UN Conference on Environment and Development (also known as the Earth Summit or Rio Conference) (1992), the outcome of which was the *Rio Declaration* and an action plan known as *Agenda 21*.[18] The *Rio Declaration* included 27 principles many of which built upon the earlier *Stockholm Declaration*. Notably, this time sustainable development was mentioned in 12 principles: 1, 4, 5, 7, 8, 9, 12, 20, 21, 22, 24 and 27. *Agenda 21* was a blueprint for action, and a brief review of the table of contents demonstrates key focus areas that each attracted a chapter devoted to them – notably energy is missing.[19]

16 *UN Declaration on the Right to Development* (UNGA Res 41/128, December 4, 1986), https://www.ohchr.org/en/instruments-mechanisms/instruments/declaration-right-development.

17 The full text can be accessed at https://sustainabledevelopment.un.org/content/documents/5987our-common-future.pdf.

18 For details of the conference, see https://www.un.org/en/conferences/environment/rio1992.

19 For the text of *Agenda 21* and all relevant outcome documents of the conference, see https://www.un.org/en/conferences/environment/rio1992.

Simultaneously, other relevant UN events focused on developmental goals with the UN Conference on Trade and Development (UNCTAD), for example, hosting various meetings from 1964 focused on developing countries in international trade. A series of UN conferences in the 1990s explored specific social issues such as human rights, women, children and nutrition, with the World Summit on Social Development adopting the *Copenhagen Declaration on Social Development* (1995), building on these previous events and commitments made.[20]

The UN has continued to host global conferences at regular intervals.[21] As will be seen in the following sections, it was at the Millennium Summit (2000) that the *Millennium Declaration* was adopted which included the wording that became the Millennium Development Goals (MDGs).[22] Later, at the UN Conference on Sustainable Development (known as 'Rio+20') (2012), member states agreed to start the process to develop the SDGs.[23]

1.3.2 Early global goals and indicators

By the turn of the 21st century, sustainable development had become a well-entrenched concept, yet it had not resulted in demonstrable advances in poverty alleviation and human rights protections for all people. This led to adoption of the *Millennium Declaration*, a non-binding global commitment to 'uphold principles of human dignity, equality and equity'.[24] The Declaration also contained wording that formed the basis of the later Millennium Development Goals, which introduced 'for the first time clear, concise and time-bound goals'.[25] The MDGs focused on poverty and hunger (MDG 1), education (MDG 2), gender equality (MDG 3), health (MDGs 4, 5 and 6), environment (MDG 7) and partnerships (MDG 8).[26] These eight goals, supported by 21 targets, were squarely focused on social progress and development, drawing explicitly on the *Universal Declaration of Human Rights*.[27]

20 For the full text, see https://www.un.org/en/development/desa/population/migration/generalassembly/docs/globalcompact/A_CONF.166_9_Declaration.pdf.

21 All of the environment and sustainable development conferences can be accessed at https://www.un.org/en/conferences/environment.

22 UN Millennium Summit, https://www.un.org/en/conferences/environment/newyork2000.

23 *UN Conference on Sustainable Development* (2012), https://www.un.org/en/conferences/environment/rio2012.

24 *Millennium Declaration* (2000), https://documents.un.org/doc/undoc/gen/n00/559/51/pdf/n0055951.pdf.

25 Bantekas and Akestoridi (2023) 513.

26 Millennium Development Goals, https://www.un.org/millenniumgoals/.

27 For the full text of the *Universal Declaration of Human Rights* (1948), see https://www.un.org/en/about-us/universal-declaration-of-human-rights.

Millennium Development Goals
Goal 1 – Eradicate extreme poverty and hunger
Goal 2 – Achieve universal primary education
Goal 3 – Promote gender equality and empower women
Goal 4 – Reduce child mortality
Goal 5 – Improve maternal health
Goal 6 – Combat HIV/AIDS, malaria and other diseases
Goal 7 – Ensure environmental sustainability
Goal 8 – Global partnership for development

The MDGs were to be achieved by 2015, but in the final MDGs Report it was noted that 'despite many successes, the poorest and most vulnerable people are being left behind'.[28] Nevertheless, it was also clear that the 'experience of the MDGs offers numerous lessons, and they will serve as the springboard for our next steps'.[29] Those next steps were the SDGs.

1.3.3 Agenda 2030 and the adoption of the SDGs

By 2012, when the Rio+20 conference was held, it had become clear that all of the MDGs would not be met by 2015 and that a refinement was needed to broaden the range of matters they covered. One vital outcome document of Rio+20 was *The Future We Want*, in which nations agreed to commence development of the SDGs and to establish the UN High-Level Political Forum on Sustainable Development (HLPF) as a central platform for them.[30] By 2015, the SDGs had been created and were adopted unanimously via a document endorsed by the UNGA: *Transforming Our World: The 2030 Agenda for Sustainable Development* ('*Agenda 2030*').[31]

The SDGs are soft law and 'define goals rather than rights'.[32] They expanded the environmental aims included in the MDGs and provided new timebound targets (to be achieved between 2015 and 2030).

28 United Nations, *The Millennium Development Goals Report 2015* (2015) 8, https://www.un.org/millenniumgoals/2015_MDG_Report/pdf/MDG%202015%20rev%20(July%201).pdf.

29 United Nations, *The Millennium Development Goals Report 2015* (2015) 9.

30 *The Future We Want* (2012), https://sustainabledevelopment.un.org/index.php?menu=1298.

31 *Agenda 2030*, https://sdgs.un.org/2030agenda.

32 Jonas Ebbesson and Ellen Hey, 'Introduction: The Sustainable Development Goals, Agenda 2030 and International Law' in J Ebbesson and E Hey (eds), *The Cambridge Handbook of The Sustainable Development Goals and International Law* (Cambridge: Cambridge University Press, 2022) 6.

The 17 SDGs

SDG 1 – End poverty in all its forms everywhere

SDG 2 – End hunger, achieve food security and improved nutrition and promote sustainable agriculture

SDG 3 – Ensure healthy lives and promote well-being for all at all ages

SDG 4 – Ensure inclusive and equitable quality education and promote lifelong learning opportunities for all

SDG 5 – Achieve gender equality and empower all women and girls

SDG 6 – Ensure availability and sustainable management of water and sanitation for all

SDG 7 – Ensure access to affordable, reliable, sustainable and modern energy for all

SDG 8 – Promote sustained, inclusive and sustainable economic growth, full and productive employment and decent work for all

SDG 9 – Build resilient infrastructure, promote inclusive and sustainable industrialization and foster innovation

SDG 10 – Reduce inequality within and among countries

SDG 11 – Make cities and human settlements inclusive, safe, resilient and sustainable

SDG 12 – Ensure sustainable consumption and production patterns

SDG 13 – Take urgent action to combat climate change and its impacts

SDG 14 – Conserve and sustainably use the oceans, seas and marine resources for sustainable development

SDG 15 – Protect, restore and promote sustainable use of terrestrial ecosystems, sustainably manage forests, combat desertification, and halt and reverse land degradation and halt biodiversity loss

SDG 16 – Promote peaceful and inclusive societies for sustainable development, provide access to justice for all and build effective, accountable and inclusive institutions at all levels

SDG 17 – Strengthen the means of implementation and revitalize the global partnership for sustainable development

Although the SDGs evolved from the MDGs, it is evident that they were also informed by international law agreements, as well as core principles and binding norms of international law. As will be seen in later chapters, the SDGs closely align with existing international law commitments. In this sense they extend and supplement treaty obligations which have traditionally not included quantified, measurable targets that are timebound.[33] Furthermore, the SDGs provide a role in integrating broad fields of international law such as human rights, trade and investment and environmental law. Many treaties operate in relative

33 There are a few exceptions to this generalisation; for example, the HCFC phase out targets and timeframes to reduce ozone-depleted substances established via the Montreal Protocol: UNEP, *About Montreal Protocol*, https://www.unep.org/ozonaction/who-we-are/about-montreal-protocol.

isolation, with separate institutions focused on implementing obligations and delivering work programmes to achieve the objectives of the treaty. The SDGs cut across these various areas and facilitate a landscape view of broad social, economic and environmental aims that are frequently embedded in these laws. These aspects are expanded upon in the section that follows.

1.4 The SDGs and international law

As noted in the previous section, the SDGs were adopted through an international politico-legal process and make numerous references to human rights law, international trade and labour conventions and other international agreements. The SDGs make explicit reference to six legally binding international instruments.[34]

In addition, several soft law developments are also mentioned, including the *Sendai Framework for Disaster Risk Reduction.* Despite the people-centred approach of the SDGs, the *Universal Declaration of Human Rights* and the human rights treaties are not named, although 'most, if not all, of the SDGs . . . relate to, and depend upon, international human rights law for their realization'.[35] Nevertheless, even where international law instruments are not directly mentioned, it is evident that the SDGs build upon global standards, rights and institutions. Chapters 2 to 8 demonstrate this point in the context of individual SDGs.

1.4.1 The status of the SDGs in international law

The SDGs are aspirational and not legally binding, meaning that the goals and targets cannot be enforced by or against any nation. The wording does not create rights or enforceable obligations, yet it has been said that they have an 'ambiguous relationship with law . . . [and their] formal status brings little clarity about their legal effects'.[36] The SDGs have been described as 'a hybrid between soft law and politics'.[37] As noted in Section 1.2, they have some 'normative effect . . . to influence and change the behaviour of states and other

34 *Agreement on Trade-Related Aspects of Intellectual Property Rights* (TRIPS), *Doha Declaration on the TRIPS Agreement and Public Health, UN Convention on the Law of the Sea, UN Framework Convention on Climate Change* (UNFCCC), World Health Organization (WHO) *Framework Convention on Tobacco Control* and World Trade Organization (WTO) agreements.

35 Ebbesson and Hey (2022), 6. Several indicators, though, do refer to international human rights law.

36 Leslie-Anne Duvic-Paoli, 'From Aspirational Politics to Soft Law? Exploring the International Legal Effects of Sustainable Development Goal 7 on Affordable and Clean Energy' (2021) 22(1) *Melbourne Journal of International Law* 1, 4.

37 Bantekas and Akestoridi (2023).

stakeholders'.[38] So they are a form of soft law, yet this should not be seen as a weakness, as instruments such as the *Universal Declaration of Human Rights*, *Stockholm Declaration* and *Rio Declaration* are all soft law documents which have had a significant global influence.

The value of non-binding initiatives such as the SDGs is that they can be ambitious and aspirational, more so than binding laws. It is not always feasible for commitments to be enforceable. As international law is made by consensus, it is unlikely that highly ambitious binding commitments will be agreed to by all nations. In addition, it is not always desirable that commitments be enforceable if they are in the nature of 'stretch targets'. Third, there may be no value in a commitment being legally binding if it will not be enforced. Few treaties are legally enforced, even though obligations may be binding. International environmental law, for example, is rarely meaningfully enforced, but in human rights there is more scope for enforcement through specialist courts. However, collective goals do not easily lend themselves to enforceability.

Although the status of the SDGs under international law is relatively clear, the role that they play is more opaque. Covering a full range of global challenges associated with achieving sustainable development, the SDGs serve the purpose of providing coherence to fragmented international laws, global policies, work programmes and agenda and providing timebound and frequently quantitative targets. Yet their effectiveness in these endeavours can only be measured in terms of progress towards the goals. Chapter 9 will explore this aspect.

1.4.2 International law and policy supporting the SDGs

Many international treaties, as well as global programs of work, have aims and objectives, yet few have quantitative goals. For example, the *Convention on Biological Diversity* (1992) objective is 'the conservation of biological diversity, the sustainable use of its components and the fair and equitable sharing of the benefits arising out of the utilization of genetic resources' (Article 1).[39] Although that instrument contains no enforceable goals or targets, the parties later adopted the soft law Aichi targets and then goals in the Kunming-Montreal Global Biodiversity Framework.[40] A rare example where enumerated goals were included in a binding instrument is climate change law and the *UN Framework Convention on Climate Change* (UNFCCC) (1992) and *Kyoto Protocol* (1997) in particular.[41] These two instruments are discussed in Chapter 7. Chapters 2 to 8 explore each SDG in detail and show

38 Scott (2022) 363.

39 See Convention on Biological Diversity (1992), www.cbd.int.

40 Convention on Biological Diversity (1992), www.cbd.int.

41 See UN Climate Change, www.unfccc.int.

how they have built on these treaty-based objects and goals in human rights, environmental, labour, trade, finance and investment laws.

1.4.3 The contribution of the SDGs to legal aims and objectives

There is no doubt that the SDGs can contribute to the objectives of international treaty regimes. Progress can be assessed qualitatively, but, as noted above, many treaties contain no specific quantitative goals or targets. In this context the SDGs have been said to 'complement the legal compliance mechanism' of international law, and together treaties and the SDGs can 'strengthen each other's compliance pull'.[42] The SDGs can also provide coherence to fragmented international law by contributing to integration.

More indirectly, the SDGs can stimulate the development of new international law. For example, the Human Rights Council (a subsidiary of the UNGA) has established a Working Group on the Right to Development and commenced work on a binding legal instrument to encapsulate the right to development.[43] Given the SDGs' strong human rights and development focus, this initiative is well aligned with the goals. In addition, the 2022 adoption of the WTO Agreement banning harmful fishery subsidies achieves the aim set out in SDG 14 (Target 14.6) and demonstrates the role that the SDGs have played in the development of international law.[44] It remains to be seen whether the SDGs can effectively contribute to the development and implementation of other international law.

1.5 An overview of the SDGs

In Section 1.3 it was explained that the SDGs evolved from earlier conference outcomes, including the MDGs. The SDGs must be considered in light of this history and in the context of pressing challenges in 2015. The sections that follow introduce the goals, targets and indicators with the details of each SDG being expanded upon in Chapters 2 to 8.

1.5.1 Social, economic and environmental goals

Agenda 2030 confirms that the SDGs comprise 17 goals, each with individual targets that 'seek to realize the human rights of all' (Preamble). To advance

42 Otto Spijkers, 'Sustainable Management of Freshwater Resources: Linking International Water Law and the Sustainable Development Goals' (2019) 28(2) *GAIA – Ecological Perspectives for Science and Society* 135–142.

43 UN Human Rights Office of the High Commissioner, *Working group on the Right to Development*, https://www.ohchr.org/en/hrc-subsidiaries/iwg-on-development.

44 WTO, *Agreement on Fisheries Subsidies,* https://www.wto.org/english/tratop_e/rulesneg_e/fish_e/fish_e.htm.

the aims of people, prosperity, peace, partnerships and the protection of the planet, the SDGs build upon existing global frameworks and the activities of international institutions. Although the SDGs do not provide a definition of sustainable development, they do enrich the concept by implicitly including a fourth pillar – security and stability – including the rule of law, peace, and the absence of conflict, transparency and accountability.[45]

The SDGs may be grouped into social goals (SDGs 1–7 and 10 on poverty, hunger, health, education, equality, water, sanitation and energy as well as equality between nations), economic development goals (SDGs 8, 9, 11 and 12 on economic growth and work, industrialisation, cities and settlements as well as consumption and production) and environmental goals (SDGs 13–15 on climate, oceans and land). In addition, there are collaborative goals that create the environment for, and facilitate the implementation of, the SDGs (SDGs 16 and 17).

Compartmentalising the SDGs in this way may not be helpful as many of them are linked, and in multiple respects they are interdependent and indivisible.[46] Furthermore, the way that the SDGs have been 'effectively transformed into a web of interconnected actions' also militates against artificially dividing them.[47] Nevertheless, this book divides the goals into logical clusters for the purpose of providing digestible chapters.

1.5.2 Targets

One of the major advances of the SDGs, vis-à-vis the MDGs, was the addition of more detailed targets, of which there are 169 in total. Whilst high-level aims add value, the detail is contained within individual targets. These targets include multiple elements necessary for the achievement of the overarching goal. Some are time limited (e.g., by 2030) and/or have a quantitative aim (e.g., to halve the number, or reduce to less than a figure or percentage, etc.). Many are purely qualitative (e.g., to improve progressively or to strengthen, etc.). Each of the 17 SDGs contains both substantive targets (numbered) and implementing measures (lettered).

A noticeable feature throughout the SDGs is a relative weakening of the ambitious high-level commitments in the headline goal to the specific targets. For example, SDG 1 seeks to 'end poverty in all its forms everywhere', and yet the targets include the commitment to 'eradicate extreme poverty; and to

45 See special issue and the introduction to it: Adamantia Rachovitsa and Marlies Hesselman, 'Introduction to the Special Issue: International Law for the Sustainable Development Goals' (2019) 2 *Brill Open Law* 1–7.
46 Bantekas and Akestoridi (2023) 534.
47 Bantekas and Akestoridi (2023) 508.

'reduce . . . by half the proportion of [people] living in poverty in all its dimensions'. This point is picked up further in Chapters 2–8.

1.5.3 Indicators

In order to measure progress on the SDGs, it is the indicators that are essential. The global indicator framework for the SDGs was adopted in 2017, after *Agenda 2030*.[48] There are currently 248 indicators, of which 231 are unique. The indicators do not measure all factors relevant to the respective target – it would not be practical to do so – but when examining progress on the SDGs it is important to understand what is being measured. Often only one or two indicators capture data on specific points, with many aspects of the target left unassessed. For example, Target 3.4 seeks to reduce premature mortality from non-communicable diseases, yet the indicators measure only mortality rates attributed to cardiovascular disease, cancer, diabetes or chronic respiratory disease and suicide (3.4.1 and 3.4.2). The indicators are divided into a tier classification system, with Tier 1 including those that are conceptually clear, with an internationally established methodology, and data is regularly produced by countries. Tier 2 are the indicators that are clear with established methodologies, but nations do not regularly produce data. Tier 3 captures those indicators where international methodologies are not currently available. The indicator framework is refined annually and comprehensively reviewed periodically, through which improvements are made.[49]

The SDG indicators are the foundation of monitoring progress, but it is the HLPF that is tasked with follow-up and review of the SDGs.[50] Progress to date and ongoing work of the HLPF are explored in Chapter 9.

1.6 Conclusion

This chapter has introduced the SDGs and outlined the background to their development and adoption. Importantly, they are squarely focused on sustainable development and add tangible goals and targets to a poorly defined concept that emerged only in the 1980s. The SDGs are far reaching and have triggered action at all levels that might not otherwise have been achieved. Yet the SDGs are not without some criticism, with scholarship suggesting that they do not 'fundamentally question the building blocks of the international economic system which are protected and maintained by "hard" law

48 UNGA, *Work of the Statistical Commission Pertaining to the 2030 Agenda for Sustainable Development* (2017), https://documents.un.org/doc/undoc/gen/n17/207/63/pdf/n1720763.pdf.

49 UN, *SDG Indicators*, https://unstats.un.org/sdgs/indicators/indicators-list/.

50 UN, *High-Level Political Forum*, https://hlpf.un.org/.

instruments and strong institutions.[51] As Chapters 2 to 8 will show, there are tensions between social, environmental and economic sustainability. For example, hunger and economic growth are in tension with environmental sustainability and economic growth in tension with income equality and decent work for all.

Undoubtedly, the SDGs supplement international law obligations by providing measurable, time-bound targets. They also provide an element of coherence across the multiple different sub-fields of international law from human rights and humanitarian law to trade, finance and investment, as well as environmental and climate change law. The SDGs provide a tangible pathway to achieving policy goals.

The chapters that follow explore groups of goals and targets in detail, as well as the indicators that support them. Chapter 2 focuses on poverty, hunger and human health, capturing the essence of SDGs 1–3. Chapter 3 also explores three social goals – gender, equity and education. Chapter 4 explores SDGs 6 and 7 with their focus on water, sanitation and energy. SDGs 8, 9 and 10 are unpacked in Chapter 5 on employment, economies and industrialisation. Cities, settlements, consumption and production feature in Chapter 6 in the context of SDGs 11 and 12. The environmental SDGs – 13, 14 and 15 – are detailed in Chapter 7. SDGs 16 and 17 are explored in Chapter 8, addressing peace, justice and partnerships. These chapters provide an advanced introduction to the SDGs before the critical analysis of progress, and how it can be enhanced, is examined in Chapter 9.

The appeal and versatility of the SDGs has led to their prioritisation across the world. Yet as their timebound end date approaches, it is imperative that a critical eye be cast over them. This book introduces, explores and explains the SDGs through an international law lens in light of their effectiveness to date and new initiatives that may be needed as we move towards and beyond 2030.

51 Ebbesson and Hey (2022) 7–8.

1
NO
POVERTY

2
ZERO
HUNGER

3
GOOD HEALTH
AND WELL-BEING

Major milestones in international human rights and global health law

Non-Binding Actions	*Date*	*Binding International Law*
Food and Agriculture Organization (FAO)	**1945**	UN Charter
First global disease tracking service	**1947**	
Universal Declaration on Human Rights World Health Organization (WHO) created	**1948**	Convention on the Prevention and Punishment of the Crime of Genocide
International Sanitary Regulations	**1951**	Convention Relating to the Status of Refugees
	1960	ILO Discrimination (Employment and Occupation) Convention (No. 111)
World Food Programme is established	**1961**	
	1965	Convention on the Elimination of All Forms of Racial Discrimination
WHO international Health Regulations	**1966**	International Covenant on Civil and Political Rights International Covenant on Economic, Social and Cultural Rights
WHO publishes first Essential Medicines List	**1977**	
FAO Plan of Action on World Food Security	**1979**	Convention on the Elimination of All Forms of Discrimination Against Women
	1984	Convention Against Torture and Other Cruel, Inhuman or Degrading Treatment or Punishment
	1989	ILO Indigenous and Tribal Peoples Convention UN Convention on the Rights of the Child
	1990	International Convention on the Protection of the Rights of All Migrant Workers
World Food Summit and Action Plan Rome Declaration on World Food Security	**1996**	
Decade for The Eradication for Poverty	**1997**	
	2003	WHO Framework Convention on Tobacco Control

(*Continued*)

(Continued)

Non-Binding Actions	*Date*	*Binding International Law*
International Health Regulations are revised	**2005**	
	2006	Convention on the Rights of Persons with Disabilities
2nd Decade for the Eradication of Poverty 2008-2017	**2008**	
Rome Declaration on World Food Security	**2009**	
WHO Pandemic Influenza Preparedness Framework	**2011**	
UN Declaration on Human Rights Education and Training		
WHO sets global targets to prevent diseases	**2012**	
Agenda 2030 and the SDGs adopted	**2015**	
UN Decade of Action on Nutrition	**2016**	
3rd Decade for the Eradication of Poverty	**2018**	
UN Declaration on universal health coverage	**2019**	
New SDG indicator on blood stream infections	**2020**	

2 Poverty, hunger and human health

SDGs 1, 2 and 3

2.1 Background

The United Nations (UN) has acknowledged that eradicating poverty is 'the greatest global challenge and an indispensable requirement of sustainable development'.[1] The causes of poverty are many and varied, including conflict, the legacy of colonialism, exploitative economic and employment conditions, weak government and governance, social exclusion and discrimination. Disease and poor health are both a source and a result of poverty,[2] and data demonstrates that over 10 per cent of the global population remained undernourished.[3] Importantly, this food insecurity is a result of poverty – not scarcity – as the global food system produces sufficient food for the world's population.[4] Reducing mortality from preventable and treatable causes, and providing universal access to health care, is critical in the context of millions of excess deaths, particularly in low- and medium-income countries.[5]

Poverty, hunger and human health are all matters that the global community has sought to address through different international organisations with varying mandates and diverse international law instruments. Eradicating poverty and hunger, for example, have long been ambitions of the United Nations and featured in the earlier Millennium Development Goals.[6] The Sustainable

1 UNGA, *Transforming Our World: The 2030 Agenda for Sustainable Development* (2015), https://sdgs.un.org/2030agenda, Preamble.
2 Advocates for International Development, *SDG 1: No Poverty – A Legal Guide* (London: Advocates for International Development (A4ID), 2023).
3 FAO, IFAD and WFP, *The State of Food Insecurity in the World 2014* (Rome: FAO, 2014) 8.
4 Carmen G Gonzalez, 'SDG2: End Hunger, Achieve Food Security and Improved Nutrition and Promote Sustainable Agriculture' in J Ebbesson and E Hey (eds), *The Cambridge Handbook of The Sustainable Development Goals and International Law* (Cambridge: Cambridge University Press, 2022) 73.
5 Margaret E Kruk et al., 'Mortality Due to Low-Quality Health Systems in the Universal Health Coverage Era: A Systematic Analysis of Amenable Deaths in 137 Countries' (2018) 392(10160) *The Lancet* 2203–2212.
6 Millennium Development Goals, https://www.un.org/millenniumgoals/.

DOI: 10.4324/9781003583981-2

Development Goals (SDGs) provide more detailed targets in these areas, recognising that greater progress is needed 'to end poverty and hunger, in all their forms and dimensions, and to ensure that all human beings can fulfil their potential in dignity and equality and in a healthy environment'.[7]

This chapter explores SDGs 1, 2 and 3 as fundamental building blocks for social sustainability. The chapter commences with the international law backdrop to these goals before examining the relevant targets and indicators. The interconnectedness of these goals with other SDGs is explored as well as the role that law can play in their achievement.

2.2 The international law and policy context

Whilst there is no legally binding commitment to eradicate poverty under international law, there was some relevant soft law prior to the SDGs.[8] For example, the UN Charter does not refer to poverty, and neither does the *Universal Declaration of Human Rights* (UDHR).[9] The *International Covenant on Economic, Social and Cultural Rights* (ICESCR) did not provide an obligation to eradicate poverty nor a right to be free of poverty yet does recognise the 'right of everyone to an adequate standard of living' (Article 11(1)). Subsequently, the Human Rights Council appointed a special rapporteur on extreme poverty and human rights[10] and in 2012 adopted a *Guiding Principle on Extreme Poverty* to assist states with poverty reduction and eradication policies.[11] Other key global organisations, such as the World Bank and the International Monetary Fund, have explicitly committed to ending extreme poverty and/or reducing poverty.[12]

In relation to SDG 2, there is no global body of food and agriculture law, although the Food and Agriculture Organisation (FAO) has the mandate to 'achieve food security for all and make sure that people have regular access to enough high-quality food to lead active, healthy lives'.[13] The UDHR includes

7 *Agenda 2030*, Preamble.

8 Dire Tladi, 'SDG1: End Poverty in All Its Forms Everywhere' in J Ebbsson and E Hey (eds), *The Cambridge Handbook of The Sustainable Development Goals and International Law* (Cambridge: Cambridge University Press, 2022) 50–71.

9 The UDHR entitles everyone to rights indispensable for dignity and equality, but it does not mention poverty.

10 UN Office of the Human Rights Commissioner, *Special Rapporteur on Extreme Poverty and Human Rights*, https://www.ohchr.org/en/special-procedures/sr-poverty.

11 A Ploska, 'All Beginnings Are Difficult: The Guiding Principles on Extreme Poverty and Human Rights a Decade After Their Adoption' (2023) 23(2) *Human Rights Law Review* 1–21.

12 World Bank Group, *Ending Poverty and Ensuring Dignity for All* (October 16, 2023), https://www.worldbank.org/en/news/feature/2023/10/16/end-poverty-and-ensure-dignity-for-all; IMF, *Support for Low-Income Countries*, https://www.imf.org/en/About/Factsheets/IMF-Support-for-Low-Income-Countries.

13 Food and Agriculture Organization of the United Nations, *About FAO*, https://www.fao.org/about/about-fao/en/.

a right to food (Article 25), supported by the ICESCR which provides a 'fundamental right of everyone to be free from hunger' and 'taking into account the problems of both food-importing and food-exporting countries, to ensure an equitable distribution of world food supplies in relation to need' (ICESCR Article 11(2)). The FAO has worked to implement the right to food including through voluntary guidelines and recommendations for governments on policy development.[14] The Human Rights Council special rapporteur on the right to food has explored the mismatch between human rights and international trade and economic law.[15] Nevertheless, international economic law has been found to undermine SDG 2 through globalisation and double standards that benefit the global north and by supporting free trade and open markets damaging to the global south.[16] Investment laws support foreign agricultural land investors at the expense of host nations and local farming communities.[17] Nevertheless, as will be seen in the following sections, several of the targets in SDG 2 are focused on growth aligned with the economic and financial SDGs and targets, which in turn are supported by economic and investment law. SDG 2 makes explicit reference to other internationally agreed-upon targets – World Health Organization (WHO) Global Targets agreed upon by member states in 2012 – focused on improving maternal, infant and child nutrition.[18]

In 1945, the UN Charter committed the UN to promoting 'solutions of international . . . health and related problems' (Art 55). In 1946 the WHO was established with the mandate 'to promote and protect the health of all peoples'.[19] The WHO Constitution defines health quite broadly as including 'a state of complete physical, mental and social well-being and not merely the absence of disease or infirmity' and notes that 'the highest attainable standard of health is one of the fundamental rights of every human being . . . [and] . . . the health of all peoples is fundamental to the attainment of peach and security' (Preamble). The WHO has thus provided a firm foundation for the inclusion of broad initiatives focused on health, not just medicine. In addition, the ICESCR recognises 'the right of everyone to the enjoyment of the highest attainable standard of physical and mental health' (Article 12). Improving health indicators was captured

14 See, for example, FAO, *Voluntary Guidelines To Support the Progressive Realization of the Right to Adequate Food in the Context of National Food Security* (2005), https://www.fao.org/policy-support/tools-and-publications/resources-details/en/c/420886/ and *Voluntary Guidelines on the Responsible Governance of Tenure of Land, Fisheries, and Forests in the Context of National Food Security* (2012), https://www.fao.org/policy-support/tools-and-publications/resources-details/en/c/416990/.

15 UNGA, *The Right to Food in the Context of International Trade Law and Policy, Interim Report of the Special Rapporteur on the Right to Food* (2020), https://digitallibrary.un.org/record/3879225?ln=en&v=pdf.

16 Gonzalez (2022) 72 and 81.

17 Gonzalez (2022) 88.

18 WHO, *Global Targets 2025: To Improve Maternal, Infant and Young Child Nutrition*, https://www.who.int/teams/nutrition-and-food-safety/global-targets-2025.

19 WHO, *Constitution of the World Health Organization* (1946), https://apps.who.int/gb/bd/PDF/bd47/EN/constitution-en.pdf?ua=1.

in Millennium Development Goals (MDGs) 4, 5 and 6, and SDG 3 builds on this history including by making explicit mention of international law: *World Health Organization Framework Convention on Tobacco Control*, *Agreement on Trade-Related Aspects of Intellectual Property Rights* and the *Doha Declaration on the TRIPS Agreement and Public Health*.

The previous short summary demonstrates the wealth of binding international law and soft law instruments that provide the backdrop to SDGs 1, 2 and 3.

2.3 SDG 1 – No poverty

Setting a time-sensitive and measurable goal to end poverty is both ambitious and bold. A common theme is the shared responsibility and need for cooperation that is evident throughout all of the SDGs. SDG 1 includes seven individual targets – those aimed at ending poverty, providing rights and protections, building resilience and implementing measures.

Goal 1. End poverty in all its forms everywhere

Targets	*Indicators*
1.1 By 2030, eradicate extreme poverty for all people everywhere, currently measured as people living on less than $1.25 a day.	*1.1.1 Proportion of the population living below the international poverty line by sex, age, employment status and geographic location (urban/rural)*
1.2 By 2030, reduce at least by half the proportion of men, women and children of all ages living in poverty in all its dimensions according to national definitions.	*1.2.1 Proportion of population living below the national poverty line, by sex and age* *1.2.2 Proportion of men, women and children of all ages living in poverty in all its dimensions according to national definitions*
1.3 Implement nationally appropriate social protection systems and measures for all, including floors, and by 2030 achieve substantial coverage of the poor and the vulnerable.	*1.3.1 Proportion of population covered by social protection floors/systems, by sex, distinguishing children, unemployed persons, older persons, persons with disabilities, pregnant women, newborns, work-injury victims and the poor and the vulnerable*
1.4 By 2030, ensure that all men and women, in particular the poor and the vulnerable, have equal rights to economic resources, as well as access to basic services, ownership and control over land and other forms of property, inheritance, natural resources, appropriate new technology and financial services, including microfinance.	*1.4.1 Proportion of population living in households with access to basic services* *1.4.2 Proportion of total adult population with secure tenure rights to land, (a) with legally recognized documentation, and (b) who perceive their rights to land as secure, by sex and type of tenure*

(*Continued*)

(Continued)

Targets	*Indicators*
1.5 By 2030, build the resilience of the poor and those in vulnerable situations and reduce their exposure and vulnerability to climate-related extreme events and other economic, social and environmental shocks and disasters.	*1.5.1 Number of deaths, missing persons and directly affected persons attributed to disasters per 100,000 population* *1.5.2 Direct economic loss attributed to disasters in relation to global gross domestic product (GDP)* *1.5.3 Number of countries that adopt and implement national disaster risk reduction strategies in line with the Sendai Framework for Disaster Risk Reduction 2015–2030* *1.5.4 Proportion of local governments that adopt and implement local disaster risk reduction strategies in line with national disaster risk reduction strategies*
1.a Ensure significant mobilization of resources from a variety of sources, including through enhanced development cooperation, in order to provide adequate and predictable means for developing countries, in particular least developed countries, to implement programmes and policies to end poverty in all its dimensions.	*1.a.1 Total official development assistance grants from all donors that focus on poverty reduction as a share of the recipient country's gross national income* *1.a.2 Proportion of total government spending on essential services (education, health and social protection)*
1.b Create sound policy frameworks at the national, regional and international levels, based on pro-poor and gender-sensitive development strategies, to support accelerated investment in poverty eradication actions.	*1.b.1 Pro-poor public social spending*

2.3.1 Ending poverty

Targets 1.1 and 1.2 do not entirely match the absolute ambition of SDG 1 itself.[20] SDG 1 has three elements: (1) ending poverty, (2) of all types and (3) in all places. Target 1.1 commits to 'eradication . . . everywhere' but only refers to 'extreme poverty', which is defined relatively weakly.[21] Target 1.2 sets a target for the 'reduction' (rather than eradication) of poverty in 'all its

20 Tladi (2022) 53.

21 The standard is set as $1.25 per day, and yet the WB defines extreme poverty as $1.90 US per day: Tladi (2022) 53.

dimensions' but only according to 'national definitions'. Yet in combination with the other targets in SDG 1, many of the underlying objectives of ending poverty – such as improving living conditions and basic services – will be advanced.

2.3.2 Providing rights and protections

Targets 1.3 and 1.4 accept that people will remain in poverty and seek to support them. Target 1.3 focuses on the provision of social protection systems for vulnerable and poor people.[22] The target focuses on improving the coverage of such systems, but the level is constrained in two respects: (1) the services are to be 'nationally appropriate' rather than of a set global standard,[23] and (2) coverage of the poor and vulnerable is to be 'substantial', which is difficult to measure.

Target 1.4 adds to the protections with the goal of providing 'to all men and women' equal rights to financial resources, services, land and property, resources and technology. This is a particularly ambitious target.

2.3.3 Building resilience

Together with reducing poverty and providing supports, Target 1.5 seeks to build resilience within the world's poor and vulnerable peoples. Notably climate-related risks, other disasters and social, economic and environmental shocks are highlighted. Presumably this would include financial crises and the effects of other events such as the COVID-19 pandemic.

2.3.4 Implementation measures

Target 1.a focuses on the mobilisation of resources – not only finance – to assist developing nations to develop and implement policies to end poverty. This target is important, as international economic law and global financial institutions tend to impose similar funding conditions on all nations, some of which have the effect of reducing services and systems that support the poor and vulnerable.[24] Target 1.b makes explicit reference to policy frameworks not only at the international level but the regional and local level too. The reference to policy could include soft law (non-binding) initiatives, although law is not mentioned.

22 The right to social security and social insurance is included in ICESCR Article 9.
23 This aligns with ICESCR's principle of progressive realisation.
24 Tladi (2022) 64.

2.4 SDG 2 – Zero hunger

This specific SDG focuses on ending hunger and builds on MDG 1, which had included one target to reduce by half the proportion of people who suffer from hunger. Interestingly, the targets do not follow the same pattern as SDG 1, although rights and protections could have been embedded in SDG 2. A review of the ten SDG 2 targets demonstrates that they include three key areas: Ending hunger and malnutrition, ensuring sustainable food production and implementing measures.

Goal 2. End hunger, achieve food security and improved nutrition and promote sustainable agriculture

Targets	*Indicators*
2.1 By 2030, end hunger and ensure access by all people, in particular the poor and people in vulnerable situations, including infants, to safe, nutritious and sufficient food all year round	*2.1.1 Prevalence of undernourishment* *2.1.2 Prevalence of moderate or severe food insecurity in the population, based on the Food Insecurity Experience Scale (FIES)*
2.2 By 2030, end all forms of malnutrition, including achieving, by 2025, the internationally agreed targets on stunting and wasting in children under 5 years of age, and address the nutritional needs of adolescent girls, pregnant and lactating women and older persons	*2.2.1 Prevalence of stunting (height for age <-2 standard deviation from the median of the World Health Organization (WHO) Child Growth Standards) among children under 5 years of age* *2.2.2 Prevalence of malnutrition (weight for height >+2 or <-2 standard deviation from the median of the WHO Child Growth Standards) among children under 5 years of age, by type (wasting and overweight)* *2.2.3 Prevalence of anaemia in women aged 15 to 49 years, by pregnancy status (percentage)*
2.3 By 2030, double the agricultural productivity and incomes of small-scale food producers, in particular women, indigenous peoples, family farmers, pastoralists and fishers, including through secure and equal access to land, other productive resources and inputs, knowledge, financial services, markets and opportunities for value addition and non-farm employment	*2.3.1 Volume of production per labour unit by classes of farming/pastoral/forestry enterprise size* *2.3.2 Average income of small-scale food producers, by sex and indigenous status*

(*Continued*)

(Continued)

Targets	*Indicators*
2.4 By 2030, ensure sustainable food production systems and implement resilient agricultural practices that increase productivity and production, that help maintain ecosystems, that strengthen capacity for adaptation to climate change, extreme weather, drought, flooding and other disasters and that progressively improve land and soil quality	*2.4.1 Proportion of agricultural area under productive and sustainable agriculture*
2.5 By 2020, maintain the genetic diversity of seeds, cultivated plants and farmed and domesticated animals and their related wild species, including through soundly managed and diversified seed and plant banks at the national, regional and international levels, and promote access to and fair and equitable sharing of benefits arising from the utilization of genetic resources and associated traditional knowledge, as internationally agreed	*2.5.1 Number of (a) plant and (b) animal genetic resources for food and agriculture secured in either medium- or long-term conservation facilities* *2.5.2 Proportion of local breeds classified as being at risk of extinction*
2.a Increase investment, including through enhanced international cooperation, in rural infrastructure, agricultural research and extension services, technology development and plant and livestock gene banks in order to enhance agricultural productive capacity in developing countries, in particular least developed countries	*2.a.1 The agriculture orientation index for government expenditures* *2.a.2 Total official flows (official development assistance plus other official flows) to the agriculture sector*
2.b Correct and prevent trade restrictions and distortions in world agricultural markets, including through the parallel elimination of all forms of agricultural export subsidies and all export measures with equivalent effect, in accordance with the mandate of the Doha Development Round	*2.b.1 Agricultural export subsidies*
2.c Adopt measures to ensure the proper functioning of food commodity markets and their derivatives and facilitate timely access to market information, including on food reserves, in order to help limit extreme food price volatility	*2.c.1 Indicator of food price anomalies*

2.4.1 Ending hunger and malnutrition

Target 2.1 provides an absolute goal of ending hunger in two respects: (1) for all people and (2) all year around by 2030. Presumably this would include in all places. Target 2.2 is also absolute in seeking to end all forms of malnutrition, with an explicit reference to the achievement of other previously agreed-upon international policy goals by 2025.[25] The achievement of these targets is linked, through SDG 2, to growth in food production despite evidence that scarcity is not the underlying cause of hunger.

2.4.2 Ensuring sustainable food production

Target 2.3 is relational and inherently linked to growth by seeking to double agricultural productivity and incomes of small-scale farmers.[26] Target 2.4 is broader, as it relates to increasing food production and productivity everywhere but is also vague by referring to ensuring sustainable production systems and unambitious in calling for the implementation of resilient agricultural practices. These two targets based on growth in food production are not fully aligned with human rights law obligations to 'ensure an equitable distribution of world food supplies in relation to need' (ICESCR Article 11(2)(b)). Target 2.5 is not focused on people but rather on the genetic diversity of seeds, plants and animals, which is linked with crop and food system resilience.

2.4.3 Implementing policy measures

The implementation targets all relate to food production, and, as with several other SDGs, Target 2.a calls for increased investment in infrastructure, research, technology and gene banks but with no quantified targets to support increased production. Target 2.b seeks to overcome part of this problem through trade restrictions and distortions in markets. Subsidies which favour large-scale commercial agriculture, predominantly in the global north, must be phased out if small-scale farmers and to be protected.[27] Yet this will not necessarily ensure livelihoods of those in the south who cannot compete in markets dominated by the north. Therefore, this target essentially continues to support trade liberalisation.[28] Target 2.c adds further to this with a focus on

25 As noted earlier, the World Health Assembly adopted a resolution endorsing a Comprehensive implementation plan on maternal, infant and young child nutrition which included six global nutrition targets to be achieved by 2025. Target 2.2 embeds two of these WHO targets.

26 This focus on small-scale food producers is matched in SDG 14, which refers to small-scale fishers.

27 Gonzalez (2022) 85.

28 Gonzalez (2022) 94.

markets which are relevant in the context of the monopolies created by the very small number of companies that dominate markets for seed, grain and agro-chemicals used in commercial agriculture.[29] Perhaps stronger obligations on developed nations are needed to create responsibilities for the global north and to address more fully the structural barriers which cause poverty and food insecurity.[30]

2.5 SDG 3 – good health and well-being

SDG 3 builds upon the separate MDGs aimed at reducing child mortality, improving maternal health and combatting global diseases. The goal includes 13 separate targets covering three substantive areas (mortality, disease and substance abuse and health services) as well as implementing measures.

Goal 3. Ensure healthy lives and promote well-being for all at all ages

Targets	*Indicators*
3.1 By 2030, reduce the global maternal mortality ratio to less than 70 per 100,000 live births	*3.1.1 Maternal mortality ratio* *3.1.2 Proportion of births attended by skilled health personnel*
3.2 By 2030, end preventable deaths of newborns and children under 5 years of age, with all countries aiming to reduce neonatal mortality to at least as low as 12 per 1,000 live births and under-5 mortality to at least as low as 25 per 1,000 live births	*3.2.1 Under-5 mortality rate* *3.2.2 Neonatal mortality rate*
3.3 By 2030, end the epidemics of AIDS, tuberculosis, malaria and neglected tropical diseases and combat hepatitis, water-borne diseases and other communicable diseases	*3.3.1 Number of new HIV infections per 1,000 uninfected population, by sex, age and key populations* *3.3.2 Tuberculosis incidence per 100,000 population* *3.3.3 Malaria incidence per 1,000 population* *3.3.4 Hepatitis B incidence per 100,000 population* *3.3.5 Number of people requiring interventions against neglected tropical diseases*

(*Continued*)

29 Gonzalez (2022) 84–85.
30 Gonzalez (2022) 94.

(Continued)

Targets	*Indicators*
3.4 By 2030, reduce by one third premature mortality from non-communicable diseases through prevention and treatment and promote mental health and well-being	*3.4.1 Mortality rate attributed to cardiovascular disease, cancer, diabetes or chronic respiratory disease* *3.4.2 Suicide mortality rate*
3.5 Strengthen the prevention and treatment of substance abuse, including narcotic drug abuse and harmful use of alcohol	*3.5.1 Coverage of treatment interventions (pharmacological, psychosocial and rehabilitation and aftercare services) for substance use disorders* *3.5.2 Alcohol per capita consumption (aged 15 years and older) within a calendar year in litres of pure alcohol*
3.6 By 2020, halve the number of global deaths and injuries from road traffic accidents	*3.6.1 Death rate due to road traffic injuries*
3.7 By 2030, ensure universal access to sexual and reproductive health-care services, including for family planning, information and education, and the integration of reproductive health into national strategies and programmes	*3.7.1 Proportion of women of reproductive age (aged 15–49 years) who have their need for family planning satisfied with modern methods* *3.7.2 Adolescent birth rate (aged 10–14 years; aged 15–19 years) per 1,000 women in that age group*
3.8 Achieve universal health coverage, including financial risk protection, access to quality essential health-care services and access to safe, effective, quality and affordable essential medicines and vaccines for all	*3.8.1 Coverage of essential health services* *3.8.2 Proportion of population with large household expenditures on health as a share of total household expenditure or income*
3.9 By 2030, substantially reduce the number of deaths and illnesses from hazardous chemicals and air, water and soil pollution and contamination	*3.9.1 Mortality rate attributed to household and ambient air pollution* *3.9.2 Mortality rate attributed to unsafe water, unsafe sanitation and lack of hygiene (exposure to unsafe Water, Sanitation and Hygiene for All (WASH) services)* *3.9.3 Mortality rate attributed to unintentional poisoning*
3.a Strengthen the implementation of the World Health Organization Framework Convention on Tobacco Control in all countries, as appropriate	*3.a.1 Age-standardized prevalence of current tobacco use among persons aged 15 years and older*

(*Continued*)

(Continued)

Targets	*Indicators*
3.b Support the research and development of vaccines and medicines for the communicable and non-communicable diseases that primarily affect developing countries, provide access to affordable essential medicines and vaccines, in accordance with the Doha Declaration on the TRIPS Agreement and Public Health, which affirms the right of developing countries to use to the full the provisions in the Agreement on Trade-Related Aspects of Intellectual Property Rights regarding flexibilities to protect public health, and, in particular, provide access to medicines for all	*3.b.1 Proportion of the target population covered by all vaccines included in their national programme* *3.b.2 Total net official development assistance to medical research and basic health sectors* *3.b.3 Proportion of health facilities that have a core set of relevant essential medicines available and affordable on a sustainable basis*
3.c Substantially increase health financing and the recruitment, development, training and retention of the health workforce in developing countries, especially in least developed countries and small island developing States	*3.c.1 Health worker density and distribution*
3.d Strengthen the capacity of all countries, in particular developing countries, for early warning, risk reduction and management of national and global health risks	*3.d.1 International Health Regulations (IHR) capacity and health emergency preparedness* *3.d.2 Percentage of bloodstream infections due to selected antimicrobial-resistant organisms*

2.5.1 Reducing mortality

The greatest focus in SDG 3 is upon reducing deaths. More than any other SDG, these targets are almost all quantified and focus on reducing mortality in specific groups of people (women and children – Targets 3.1 and 3.2) and decreasing deaths by cause (e.g., non-communicable diseases, road traffic accidents, hazardous chemicals and pollution – Targets 3.3, 3.4, 3.6 and 3.9). Only the last of these is not quantified, with the aim being substantial reduction. This specificity perhaps reflects the fact that three MDGs covered these aims.

2.5.2 Combatting diseases and substance abuse

An absolute goal is set of ending epidemics, with only a commitment to combat other diseases (Target 3.3.). Target 3.5 is weaker still in seeking to strengthen prevention and treatment of drug and alcohol abuse.

2.5.3 Increasing health services

Target 3.7 seeks to facilitate the provision of reproductive health services and is aligned with Target 3.8, which focuses on the provision of universal health coverage. Target 3.8 is particularly ambitious in seeking to achieve safe, effective, quality and affordable health coverage for all people.

2.5.4 Implementing measures

Targets 3.a and 3.b include some of the limited mentions of specific global instruments/agreements. Target 3.c focuses on enhancing the health workforce through financing and training and 3.d on strengthening capacity building measures to improve management of health risks.

2.6 Progressing SDGs 1, 2 and 3

In order to achieve the ambitious goals of SDGs 1, 2 and 3, the synergies between them, and indeed their alignment with other goals, must be garnered. As explored below, there are some inherent tensions which must be taken into account. Furthermore, as outlined in Section 2.2, there is a wealth of international law obligations underpinning these SDGs, and law and policy can also play a role in achieving the targets. Both of these matters are discussed in the following sections.

2.6.1 Linkages across the SDGs[31]

The clearest connections are between SDGs 1, 2 and 3. For example, poverty and food insecurity are clear, as is the interconnectedness of poverty, health and well-being. There is a general weakening of the ambition of the three goals in the targets within each. The broad ambition of SDG 3 and the goal of health and well-being for all at all ages is not matched in the targets, with the elderly, for example, not being directly mentioned at all. There is also inconsistent reference to pre-existing global obligations, with SDG 3 referring explicitly to several international law conventions, which is not matched in SDGs 1 and 2.

Education is clearly critical to ending poverty (SDG 4), as is the goal of reducing inequality (SDG 10). Gender equality (SDG 5) is aligned with the targets in SDG 2 (given that women produce 50 per cent of the world's food and have a greater percentage of responsibility for preparing and cooking

31 For a broader examination of linkages with SDGs 2 and 3, see International Council for Science, *A Guide to SDG Interaction=s: From Science to Implementation* (2017), https://council.science/wp-content/uploads/2017/05/SDGs-Guide-to-Interactions.pdf.

food) and SDG 3 including reducing maternal mortality. Access to clean water, sanitation and energy are significant too (SDGs 6 and 7). Having decent work and employment (SDG 8), resilient infrastructure (SDG 9) and sustainable settlements (SDG 11) will both be advanced by and support the achievement of SDGs 1–3. In addition, equality amongst nations (SDG 10) and sustainable consumption and production (SDG 11) are directly relevant to poverty, health and food security. Less clear, but still relevant to poverty, hunger and health are SDGs 13, 14 and 15 on combatting climate change and securing environmental health, which are needed for food production as well as well-being – notably Indicators 1.5.1, 1.5.3 and 1.5.4 are identical to 13.1.1, 13.1.2 and 13.1.3, respectively. SDG 14 refers to fisheries of relevance to reducing hunger and poverty. Furthermore, SDGs 14 and 15 include some species and biodiversity targets which could provide support for SDG 2 Target 2.5 on genetic diversity needed for sustainable agriculture and food production. SDGs 16 (peace, justice and strong institutions) will be advanced if SDGs 1–3 are met, and SDG 17 on global partnerships is clearly necessary to support global food systems and address global health risks.

2.6.2 The role of law and policy

Law is specifically referred to as a measure in Indicator 1.4.2. Creating and implementing policies feature in Targets 1.a and 1.b. As noted in section 2.5.4, international treaties are specifically named in Targets 3.a and Indicator 3.d.1.

Human rights and health law are critical to the achievement of much of SDGs 1, 2 and 3. Property law is relevant to Targets 1.4 and 2.3, and legal frameworks would also be relevant to goals such as reducing road deaths (Target 3.6) and preventing substance abuse (Target 3.5). Investment law can assist poverty reduction as well as food security.[32] International economic law principally supports wealth creation, which should have a positive influence on ending poverty, and international trade law supports free trade through bodies such as the World Trade Organization (WTO) aimed at providing 'a more inclusive trading system'.[33] Nevertheless, scholars have queried whether free trade is the best way to end poverty given inequities between nations that prevent developing countries being able to compete in global marketplaces.[34]

32 S Dhahri and A Omri, 'Are International Capital Flows Really Matter for Achieving SDGs 1 and 2: Ending Poverty and Hunger?' (2020) 156 *Review of World Economics* 731–767.

33 WTO, *What We Stand For,* https://www.wto.org/english/thewto_e/whatis_e/what_stand_for_e.htm.

34 For a summary of this scholarship, see Tladi (2022) 62.

2.7 Conclusion

Poverty, hunger and human health lie at the heart of 'people', highlighted in *Agenda 2030* as a focus of the SDGs. Many of the targets draw heavily on the earlier MDGs and the work of relevant UN bodies such as the FAO and WHO and are supported by human rights law. The connection with economics, trade and investment is evident throughout these SDGs, and yet this is not uncontroversial. It remains to be seen whether financial arrangements truly support or undermine the ambitious goals. Despite progress being made on the majority of SDGs 1, 2 and 3, there has been regression in some areas, and the more ambitious targets may not be met.[35] Furthermore, the UN High Level Political Forum on Sustainable Development (HLPF) expressed concern about 'continued poverty and widening inequalities . . . that are pushing our world to the brink . . . [and] food security and nutrition . . . challenges are derailing progress on the Sustainable Development Goals'[36] and that 'cascading global crises have highlighted and exacerbated existing . . . unequal access to healthcare'.[37] These statements demonstrate much work remains to be done before 2030.

35 UNGA, *Progress Towards the Sustainable Development Goals* (2024), https://unstats.un.org/sdgs/files/report/2024/SG-SDG-Progress-Report-2024-advanced-unedited-version.pdf. See also Our World in Data, *SDG Tracker: Measuring Progress Towards the Sustainable Development Goals*, https://ourworldindata.org/sdgs.

36 UNGA, *Political Declaration of the High-Level Political Forum on Sustainable Development Convened Under the Auspices of the General Assembly* (2023), para 25.

37 UNGA, *Political Declaration of the High-Level Political Forum on Sustainable Development Convened Under the Auspices of the General Assembly* (2023), para 27.

Timeline of key developments relating to gender, equity and education

Non-Binding Actions	*Date*	*Binding International Law*
UN Educational, Scientific and Cultural Organization (UNESCO) is founded	**1945**	Charter of the United Nations
Universal Declaration on Human Rights	**1948**	
	1951	ILO Convention No. 100: Equal Remuneration
	1953	Convention on the Political Rights of Women

(*Continued*)

(Continued)

Non-Binding Actions	*Date*	*Binding International Law*
	1957	Convention on the Nationality of Married Women
	1960	UNESCO Convention against Discrimination in Education
	1965	International Convention on the Elimination of All Forms of Racial Discrimination
	1966	International Covenant on Economic, Social and Cultural Rights
Decade to Combat Racism and Racial Discrimination	**1973**	
UNESCO Recommendation concerning Education for International Understanding, Co-operation and Peace Education relating to Human Rights and Fundamental Freedoms	**1974**	
	1979	Convention on the Elimination of all Forms of Discrimination against Women
	1989	Convention on the Rights of the Child
World Declaration for Education for All and Framework for Action to Meet Basic Learning Needs	**1990**	International Convention on the Protection of the Rights of All Migrant Workers and Members of Their Families
UN Declaration on Violence against Women	**1992**	
Declaration on the Elimination of Violence Against Women	**1993**	
Decade for Human Rights Education	**1995**	
Beijing Declaration and Platform for Action		
	1999	ILO Convention no. 182 on the Worst Forms of Child Labour
	2000	Protocol to Prevent, Suppress and Punish Trafficking in Persons Especially Women and Children

(*Continued*)

(Continued)

Non-Binding Actions	*Date*	*Binding International Law*
UN Literacy Decade: Education for All	**2003**	
UN Decade of Education for Sustainable Development	**2005**	
UNESCO Global Alliance to Monitor Learning created	**2006**	Convention on the Rights of Persons with Disabilities
UNICEF Early Childhood Development Index introduced	**2009**	
Agenda 2030 and the SDGs adopted	**2015**	
Incheon Declaration for Education 2030 and the Education 2030 Framework for Action		
Abidjan Principles on the Right to Education	**2019**	

3 Gender, equity and education

SDGs 4 and 5

3.1 Background

Agenda 2030 envisions 'a world with universal literacy . . . [and] equitable and universal access to quality education at all levels' (para 7) and 'respect for . . . equality and non-discrimination' where 'every woman and girl enjoys full gender equality . . . and barriers to their empowerment have been removed' (para 8). Education and gender equality contribute to both the 'People' and 'Prosperity' elements of *Agenda 2030* (Preamble). Gender equality is a fundamental human right and has long been recognised in international law. Although progress has been made in many areas some indicators are worsening.[1] Education is also a fundamental human right, essential for people to fully participate in society.[2] Although perhaps not conceived of as an essential need in the way that food and water are, it is critically important to development, livelihoods and therefore poverty eradication. A significant proportion of the world's population have not had access to basic education, and many remain illiterate.

In relation to education, MDG 2 focused on enrolment and ensuring completion of primary schooling and literacy rates. MDG Target 3.A added to this by seeking to eliminate gender disparity in primary and secondary education. Despite progress being made from 2000 until 2015, none of the MDG targets related to education were met. As will be seen, SDG 4 goes much further in terms of the breadth of education, skill-building and schooling included that support life-long learning, and the focus on quality. Progress has again been made since 2015, although with the closure of schools during the COVID-19

1 UN SDGs, *Goal 5: Achieve Gender Equality and Empower All Women and Girls*, https://www.un.org/sustainabledevelopment/gender-equality/.

2 For further information on the impact of educating girls, see: UN, *Educate Girls, Eradicate Poverty – A Mutually Reinforcing Goal*, https://www.un.org/en/chronicle/article/educate-girls-eradicate-poverty-mutually-reinforcing-goal.

DOI: 10.4324/9781003583981-3

pandemic, education rates fell.[3] MDG 3 was similarly limited in its targets on gender equity, which have been expanded in SDG 5.

This chapter explores SDGs 4 and 5 together because, although they are separate issues, both gender equity and quality education contribute to social sustainability and development more broadly. The chapter commences by explaining the international legal backdrop to these goals, before examining the detail of the SDGs, targets and indicators, and the role that law and policy can play moving forward.

3.2 The international law and policy context

There is a wealth of international law that underpins SDGs 4 and 5. The United Nations (UN) Charter (1945) sets out the purposes of the UN, including to promote and encourage 'respect for human rights and for fundamental freedoms for all without distinction as to race, sex, language, or religion' (Article 1(3)). The *Universal Declaration on Human Rights* (1948) sets out principles of equality and non-discrimination (Articles 1 and 2) and was the first legal instrument to recognise that everyone has the right to education (Article 26). It is the UN Educational, Scientific and Cultural Organization (UNESCO) that has the global mandate to advance education. The later *UNESCO Convention against Discrimination in Education* (1960) includes binding obligations that require state parties to ensure free primary education and access to secondary and tertiary education, with everyone having equal right to that education free from discrimination. Article 13 of the *International Covenant on Economic, Social and Cultural Rights* (1966) sets out that human rights must be equally enjoyed by men and women (Article 3) and that everyone has the right to just and favourable work conditions including equal opportunities and remuneration for work of equal value (Article 7) and expands on the rights to education. Simultaneously the *International Covenant on Civil and Political Rights* (1966) (ICCPR) requires all state parties to ensure the rights in the covenant are enjoyed equally by men and women (Article 3). The ICCPR also includes provisions aimed at eliminating forced marriage (Article 23). The *Convention on the Elimination of all Forms of Discrimination against Women* (1979) also supports the right to education and focuses on the elimination of discrimination to ensure that women and girls have equal opportunities to the same quality and type of education as men and boys (Article 10). The right to be free from discrimination and to have access to education also feature in the *International Convention on the Elimination of All Forms of Racial Discrimination* (1965), *Convention on the Rights of the Child* (1989), *International Convention on the Protection of the Rights of All Migrant Workers*

3 Advocates for International Development, *SDG 4: Quality Education – A Legal Guide* (London: A4ID, 2022) 6.

and Members of Their Families (1990) and the *Convention on the Rights of Persons with Disabilities* (2006). More recent developments include the *Incheon Declaration and Framework for Action for the Implementation of SDG 4* (2015) and the *Abidjan Principles on the Right to Education* (2019), the latter setting out ten overarching principles relating to the provision and regulation of education, financing, accountability and monitoring.[4] In 1998 a UN Special Rapporteur on the right to education was established and has submitted reports to the Human Rights Council.[5]

Clearly, international legal instruments provide a foundation for rights to equality and education. Nevertheless, international human rights law leaves it to states to decide how to implement these rights, and so the legal frameworks and regulations relating to education, for example, are mostly found at the domestic level.[6] Furthermore, as will be seen in the following, the SDGs do go further than international law in several respects.[7]

3.3 SDG 4 – quality education

SDG covers all levels and types of education from early childhood learning, schooling and tertiary and vocational education essential for lifelong learning – although this term is not defined. A scan of the targets and indicators demonstrates a strong focus on equity, quality and inclusiveness, common across the SDGs. The SDG 4 targets can be divided into access to education, learning outcomes and implementation measures, each of which is explored in the sections that follow.

Goal 4. Ensure inclusive and equitable quality education and promote lifelong learning opportunities for all

Targets	*Indicators*
4.1 By 2030, ensure that all girls and boys complete free, equitable and quality primary and secondary education leading to relevant and effective learning outcomes	*4.1.1 Proportion of children and young people (a) in grades 2/3; (b) at the end of primary; and (c) at the end of lower secondary achieving at least a minimum proficiency level in (i) reading and (ii) mathematics, by sex* *4.1.2 Completion rate (primary education, lower secondary education, upper secondary education)*

(*Continued*)

4 The Abidjan Principles on the Right to Education, https://www.abidjanprinciples.org/.

5 UN Human Rights, *Officer of the High Commissioner, Special Rapporteur on the Right to Education*, https://www.ohchr.org/en/special-procedures/sr-education.

6 Fons Coomans, 'SDG 4: Ensure Inclusive and Equitable Quality Education and Promote Lifelong Learning Opportunities for All' in J Ebbesson and E Hey (eds), *The Cambridge Handbook of the Sustainable Development Goals and International Law* (Cambridge: Cambridge University Press, 2022) 118.

7 For further discussion, see Coomans (2022).

(Continued)

Targets	*Indicators*
4.2 By 2030, ensure that all girls and boys have access to quality early childhood development, care and pre-primary education so that they are ready for primary education	*4.2.1 Proportion of children aged 24–59 months who are developmentally on track in health, learning and psychosocial well-being, by sex* *4.2.2 Participation rate in organized learning (one year before the official primary entry age), by sex*
4.3 By 2030, ensure equal access for all women and men to affordable and quality technical, vocational and tertiary education, including university	*4.3.1 Participation rate of youth and adults in formal and non-formal education and training in the previous 12 months, by sex*
4.4 By 2030, substantially increase the number of youth and adults who have relevant skills, including technical and vocational skills, for employment, decent jobs and entrepreneurship	*4.4.1 Proportion of youth and adults with information and communications technology (ICT) skills, by type of skill*
4.5 By 2030, eliminate gender disparities in education and ensure equal access to all levels of education and vocational training for the vulnerable, including persons with disabilities, indigenous peoples and children in vulnerable situations	*4.5.1 Parity indices (female/male, rural/urban, bottom/top wealth quintile and others such as disability status, indigenous peoples and conflict-affected, as data become available) for all education indicators on this list that can be disaggregated*
4.6 By 2030, ensure that all youth and a substantial proportion of adults, both men and women, achieve literacy and numeracy	*4.6.1 Proportion of population in a given age group achieving at least a fixed level of proficiency in functional (a) literacy and (b) numeracy skills, by sex*
4.7 By 2030, ensure that all learners acquire the knowledge and skills needed to promote sustainable development, including, among others, through education for sustainable development and sustainable lifestyles, human rights, gender equality, promotion of a culture of peace and non-violence, global citizenship and appreciation of cultural diversity and of culture's contribution to sustainable development	*4.7.1 Extent to which (i) global citizenship education and (ii) education for sustainable development are mainstreamed in (a) national education policies; (b) curricula; (c) teacher education; and (d) student assessment*
4.a Build and upgrade education facilities that are child, disability and gender sensitive and provide safe, non-violent, inclusive and effective learning environments for all	4.a.1 Proportion of schools offering basic services, by type of service

(*Continued*)

(Continued)

Targets	*Indicators*
4.b By 2020, substantially expand globally the number of scholarships available to developing countries, in particular least developed countries, small island developing States and African countries, for enrolment in higher education, including vocational training and information and communications technology, technical, engineering and scientific programmes, in developed countries and other developing countries	*4.b.1 Volume of official development assistance flows for scholarships by sector and type of study*
4.c By 2030, substantially increase the supply of qualified teachers, including through international cooperation for teacher training in developing countries, especially least developed countries and small island developing States	*4.c.1 Proportion of teachers with the minimum required qualifications, by education level*

3.3.1 Access to education

The focus on providing equitable access to quality education can be seen in Targets 4.1, 4.2, 4.3, 4.4 and 4.5. Notably, early childhood and pre-primary education is not included in other international instruments.[8] Whilst equity and quality are mentioned throughout, only 'free' education is mentioned in Target 4.1 in relation to primary and secondary schooling, and 'affordable' only features in Target 4.3 on technical, vocational and tertiary education. The indicators are largely focused on proportions of children and/or the population and participation rates, although 4.1.1(c) measures proficiency in reading and mathematics and Indicator 4.4.1 information and communications technology skills. Target 4.5 measures data and indices but does not track anti-discrimination laws, policies and practices – although these feature elsewhere in the SDGs.

3.3.2 Learning outcomes

Target 4.6 is about the achievement of critical skills – numeracy and literacy – measured in Indicator 4.6.1 as a proportion of the population with proficiency. Knowledge and skills more directly related to sustainable development are the focus on Target 4.7, although the indicator measures policies and curricula rather than the proportion of learners achieving a certain proficiency

8 Coomans (2022) 120.

level. Indicators 4.6.1 and 4.1.1(c) measure proficiency in numeracy and literacy, and a similar approach could be taken for Target 4.7. However, there are no globally agreed standards or methodologies for such proficiency levels and measuring sustainability skills would be challenging.[9]

3.3.3 Implementation measures

The targets on implementation include educational facilities (4.a), scholarships (4.b) and teaching staff (4.c). No reference is made to international education and student mobility, nor education as a commodity, the role of private actors or the connected trade and investment related aspects.

3.4 SDG 5 – gender equality

A specific SDG focused on equality, and empowerment of women and girls in particular, is an important inclusion and expands beyond MDG 3. The sections that follow are divided based on the various focus areas of the targets: ending discrimination, enabling environments and implementation measures.

Goal 5. Achieve gender equality and empower all women and girls

Targets	*Indicators*
5.1 End all forms of discrimination against all women and girls everywhere	*5.1.1 Whether or not legal frameworks are in place to promote, enforce and monitor equality and non-discrimination on the basis of sex*
5.2 Eliminate all forms of violence against all women and girls in the public and private spheres, including trafficking and sexual and other types of exploitation	*5.2.1 Whether or not legal frameworks are in place to promote, enforce and monitor equality and non-discrimination on the basis of sex* *5.2.2 Proportion of women and girls aged 15 years and older subjected to sexual violence by persons other than an intimate partner in the previous 12 months, by age and place of occurrence*
5.3 Eliminate all harmful practices, such as child, early and forced marriage and female genital mutilation	*5.3.1 Proportion of women aged 20–24 years who were married or in a union before age 15 and before age 18* *5.3.2 Proportion of girls and women aged 15–49 years who have undergone female genital mutilation, by age*

(*Continued*)

9 Advocates for International Development, *SDG 4* (2022) 6 and 12.

(Continued)

Targets	*Indicators*
5.4 Recognize and value unpaid care and domestic work through the provision of public services, infrastructure and social protection policies and the promotion of shared responsibility within the household and the family as nationally appropriate	*5.4.1 Proportion of time spent on unpaid domestic and care work, by sex, age and location*
5.5 Ensure women's full and effective participation and equal opportunities for leadership at all levels of decision-making in political, economic and public life	*5.5.1 Proportion of seats held by women in (a) national parliaments and (b) local governments* *5.5.2 Proportion of women in managerial positions*
5.6 Ensure universal access to sexual and reproductive health and reproductive rights as agreed in accordance with the Programme of Action of the International Conference on Population and Development and the Beijing Platform for Action and the outcome documents of their review conferences	*5.6.1 Proportion of women aged 15–49 years who make their own informed decisions regarding sexual relations, contraceptive use and reproductive health care* *5.6.2 Number of countries with laws and regulations that guarantee full and equal access to women and men aged 15 years and older to sexual and reproductive health care, information and education*
5.a Undertake reforms to give women equal rights to economic resources, as well as access to ownership and control over land and other forms of property, financial services, inheritance and natural resources, in accordance with national laws	5.a.1 (a) Proportion of total agricultural population with ownership or secure rights over agricultural land, by sex; and (b) share of women among owners or rights-bearers of agricultural land, by type of tenure 5.a.2 Proportion of countries where the legal framework (including customary law) guarantees women's equal rights to land ownership and/or control
5.b Enhance the use of enabling technology, in particular information and communications technology, to promote the empowerment of women	5.b.1 Proportion of individuals who own a mobile telephone, by sex
5.c Adopt and strengthen sound policies and enforceable legislation for the promotion of gender equality and the empowerment of all women and girls at all levels	*5.c.1 Proportion of countries with systems to track and make public allocations for gender equality and women's empowerment*

3.4.1 Ending discrimination

Target 5.1 focuses squarely on ending discrimination for all women and girls everywhere. Yet the indicator only measures legal frameworks in place. Target 5.5 is about ensuring full and effective participation in political, economic and public life. Again the indicator is narrowed to the number of women in government (5.5.1) and in managerial positions (5.5.2). Other areas of public and economic life are not measured.

3.4.2 Enabling environments

Targets 5.2 and 5.3 focus on eliminating harmful practices including ending violence, forced marriage and genital mutilation. Indicators 5.2.1 and 5.2.2 are mis-aligned in coverage, with the former relating to all forms of violence but the latter only measuring sexual violence. Targets 5.4 and 5.6 seek to build more enabling environments for gender equity by recognising unpaid work and ensuring universal access to reproductive health. Indicator 5.4.1 measures time spent on unpaid work rather than measuring the policies and strategies the value that work, significantly narrowing the focus.

3.4.3 Implementation measures

To achieve SDG 5, Targets 5.a and 5.c focus on law and policy that supports equal rights for women, gender equality and empowerment. The indicators relate only to ownership of land, with 5.a.1 relating only to agricultural land. Indicator 5.a.2 measures legal frameworks but again only in relation to land ownership, which significantly narrows the equity matters being tracked. Target 5.b is about the use of technology, with the indicator referring to ownership of mobile telephones.

3.5 Progressing SDGs 4 and 5

Social sustainability is one of the pillars of sustainable development, and education and equality are central to its achievement.

3.5.1 Mutual support across the SDGs

SDGs 4 and 5 are interlinked, as discrimination and gender inequality (the focus of SDG 5) undermine the achievement of equal access to education for all (Target 4.5), and empowered women and children can take full advantage of and contribute to education. Target 4.a specifically highlights the need for educational facilities that are 'gender sensitive', safe and non-violent. Indicator 5.6.2 records the number of nations with laws that guarantee full access to education.

Disparities in wealth are a major hurdle to achieving equitable education, and in turn poor education makes it challenging to move out of poverty, linking SDGs 4 and 1.[10] Similarly, knowledge and understanding of health risks

10 Advocates for International Development, *SDG 4* (2022) 9.

(SDG 3) may be impacted by poor education. Vocational education is also relevant to SDG 2, as farming and agricultural knowledge and skills are important for food production. Formal education is critical for many other SDGs, as education allows an individual to contribute more fully to communities, and societies benefit from an educated population. Skill-building is needed to advance SDG 8 on productivity, growth and full employment (see Target 8.6 in particular), SDG 9 relating to industrialisation and innovation and SDG 10 on sustainable consumption and production. The skills needed for the energy transition (SDG 7), to achieve sustainable production and consumption (SDG 12 and Indicator 12.8.1 in particular) and to combat climate change (SDG 13, with Target 13.3 specifically referring to education) and address the biodiversity crisis (SDGs 14 and 15) also depend on education and skill-building. The provision of education is dependent upon government funding, frequently generated through taxes, and so the achievement of SDG 4 is linked with Target 17.1, and Indicator 1.a.2 captures government spending on education services. Targets 12.8 and 13.3 refer explicitly to information, education and awareness-raising.

Gender equality and anti-discrimination feature not only in SDG 5 but also in SDG 10 in relation to inequality between nations and in SDG 16 on laws and policies for sustainable development. Women are also explicitly referred to in targets under SDGs 1, 2, 6, 8, 11 and 13. However, despite the fundamental nature of gender equality, it is not referred to in all other SDGs.[11] Although SDG 5 does not engage directly with broader LGBTQI+ issues, in combination with SDG 10, the aim is to eliminate all discrimination. For example, Target 10.2 specifically seeks to 'empower and promote the . . . inclusion of all, irrespective of . . . sex . . . or other status'.

3.5.2 The role of law and policy

Law and policy have a significant role to play in setting the agenda for education and providing the foundation for equitable access and outcomes. No specific laws or conventions are mentioned in these two SDGs, although Target 5.6 refers to the *Programme of Action of the International Conference on Population and Development* and the *Beijing Platform for Action*. Target 5.c is squarely focused on law and policy for the promotion of gender quality and empowerment of women and girls. However, Target 5.a and Indicators 5.1.1, 5.6.2 and 5.a.2 capture the existence of laws and legal frameworks supporting non-discrimination. Indicator 4.7.1 explicitly measures the extent to

11 Patricia Kameri-Mbote and Nkatha Kabira, 'SDG 5: Achieve Gender Equality and Empower All Women and Girls' in J Ebbsson and E Hey (eds), *The Cambridge Handbook of The Sustainable Development Goals and International Law* (Cambridge: Cambridge University Press, 2022) 142.

which national education policies include global citizenship and sustainable development education (and this indicator is identical to 12.8.1 and 13.3.1), and Target 5.4 seeks to advance the recognition of unpaid and domestic work in social protection policies.

3.6 Conclusion

SDGs 4 and 5 are vital for social sustainability and therefore for the achievement of the SDGs as a whole. Progress on both SDGs is lagging, with less than a third of the targets on track and likely to be met by 2030.[12] On a more positive note, completion of primary and lower secondary education continued to improve. As two longstanding goals of the global community underpinned by many international law instruments, efforts must continue to advance education and equality for all.

12 UNGA, *Progress Towards the Sustainable Development Goals* (2024), https://unstats.un.org/sdgs/files/report/2024/SG-SDG-Progress-Report-2024-advanced-unedited-version.pdf. See also Our World in Data, *SDG Tracker: Measuring Progress Towards the Sustainable Development Goals* (2023), https://ourworldindata.org/sdgs.

Timeline of key developments in water, sanitation and energy

Soft Initiatives	*Date*	*Binding Legal Instruments*
Universal Declaration on Human Rights	**1948**	
	1966	International Covenant on Economic, Social and Cultural Rights
	1973	Ramsar Convention on Wetlands of International Importance
Mar Del Plata Action Plan	**1977**	
	1979	Convention on the Elimination of all Forms of Discrimination against Women
International Drinking Water Supply and Sanitation Decade	**1981**	

(*Continued*)

(Continued)

Soft Initiatives	*Date*	*Binding Legal Instruments*
	1989	Convention on the Rights of the Child
Energy Charter Declaration	**1991**	
	1992	Convention on the Protection and Use of Transboundary Watercourses and International Lakes UN Framework Convention on Climate Change Convention on Biological Diversity
	1994	UN Convention to Combat Desertification Energy Charter Treaty Convention on Nuclear Safety
	1997	Kyoto Protocol
	1998	Protocol on Energy Efficiency and Related Environmental Aspects
UN Resolution on the Right to Development	**1999**	Protocol on Water and Health
	2004	Berlin Rules on Water Resources
International Decade for Action, "Water for Life"	**2005**	
	2006	Convention on the Rights of Persons with Disabilities
UN Resolution 7/22 on the Human Right to Safe and Clean Drinking Water and Sanitation ILA Draft Articles on the Law of Transboundary Aquifers	**2008**	
UN Resolution 64/292 the Human right to Water and Sanitation	**2010**	
UN Sustainable Energy for All (SEforALL) initiative	**2011**	
UNGA Resolution on Promotion of new and renewable sources of energy	**2012**	
UN Decade of Sustainable Energy for All 2014-2024	**2014**	
Agenda 2030 and the SDGs UN Resolution on the Right to Safe Drinking Water and Sanitation	**2015**	Paris Agreement International Energy Charter
International Decade for Action "Water for Sustainable Development" (2018-2028)	**2018**	

4 Water, sanitation and energy

SDGs 6 and 7

4.1 Background

Water is critical for life on Earth. It provides myriad natural functions as well as services essential for human societies. Yet the majority of water on Earth is found in the ocean, and only 3 per cent is freshwater, of which almost two thirds is ice, permafrost or found deep underground. Therefore, although it is a renewable resource, freshwater stocks are limited. Managing freshwater resources has been a challenge for thousands of years, with access, property rights, pollution, floods and droughts all being water-related concerns. The most pressing issue for social sustainability is clean drinking water and adequate sanitation, as billions of people live without these, and significant numbers of people die from water-related diseases each year. The disposal and dumping of waste in ways that pollute freshwater is another challenge that hinders the provision of safe drinking water and impacts other species and ecosystems.

Energy is another social sustainability challenge, as it is required for basic needs such as cooking food, heating, transportation and electricity production.[1] Millions of people remain without access to electricity, for example.[2] Energy is also needed to drive economic growth and development, and yet these can also contribute to environmental damage. Climate change, for example, is largely attributable to unsustainable energy production from fossil fuels, and billions of people continue to rely upon other polluting energy sources (coal, charcoal, wood, crop waste, animal dung, kerosene, etc.), with environmental and health impacts.[3] Energy thus exemplifies the need to balance social and developmental goals with environmental concerns. Whilst progress has been made in some parts of the world and for some fuel sources (reductions in coal and kerosene

1 Advocates for International Development, *SDG 7: Affordable and Clean Energy – A Legal Guide* (London: A4ID, 2024) 4.

2 UNGA, *Progress Towards the Sustainable Development Goals* (2024), https://unstats.un.org/sdgs/files/report/2024/SG-SDG-Progress-Report-2024-advanced-unedited-version.pdf. Advocates for International Development, *SDG 7* (2024) 4.

3 Advocates for International Development, *SDG 7* (2024).

DOI: 10.4324/9781003583981-4

use) in some regions, energy production remains a critical challenge. In developed nations, energy transitions to renewables can be seen for electricity production but less so for heating and transportation.[4]

The global community sought to address access to water and sanitation in the Millennium Development Goals. Importantly, MDG 7 was met as the proportion of the global population without access to safe water was halved, yet 30 per cent of the world's population remain without access to safe drinking water at home.[5] SDG 6 thus goes further in seeking universal access to safe drinking water. In contrast, energy was not included at all in the MDGs – and governments been reluctant to work cooperatively on energy matters – therefore SDG 7 adds significantly to global goals and targets.[6]

This chapter explores SDGs 6 and 7 together, given the nature of water and energy for basic human needs. The chapter commences by explaining the international legal backdrop to these goals before examining the detail of the SDGs, targets and indicators and the role that they play in addressing the challenges confronting us.

4.2 The international law and policy context

Freshwater (rivers, lakes, aquifers, etc.) and conventional energy sources (coal, wood, oil and gas reserves, etc.) are found within national borders and so are subject to sovereignty, meaning that states can manage them as they wish. Nevertheless, international human rights, trade and investment, developmental, environmental and natural resources law are relevant to SDGs 6 and 7. Neither the *Universal Declaration of Human Rights* (1948) nor the later *International Covenant on Economic, Social and Cultural Rights* (1966) (ICESCR) explicitly recognise a right to water, sanitation or energy. Nevertheless, the ICESCR includes the right to an adequate standard of living, adequate food and continuous improvement in living conditions (Article 11). These have been interpreted as including a human right to water and sanitation,[7] but no similar recognition has been given to energy. The *Convention on the Rights of the Child* (1989) includes a right to 'enjoyment of the highest attainable standard of health' (Article 24), which is directly relevant to the provision of access to water, sanitation and energy. The *Convention on the Elimination of All Forms of Discrimination against Women* (1979) is

4 Advocates for International Development, *SDG 7* (2024) 7.

5 Advocates for International Development, *SDG 6: Clean Water and Sanitation* (London: A4ID, 2022) 4.

6 Leslie-Anne Duvic-Paoli, 'From Aspirational Politics to Soft Law? Exploring the International Legal Effects of Sustainable Development Goal 7 on Affordable and Clean Energy' (2021) 22(1) *Melbourne Journal of International Law* 1–23.

7 UN Water, *Human Rights to Water and Sanitation*, www.unwater.org/water-facts/human-rights-water-and-sanitation.

more explicit, providing 'all women in rural areas the right to adequate living conditions in relation to sanitation and water supply . . . [and] electricity supply' (Article 14). More recently the UN has adopted three relevant resolutions: UN Resolution 7/22 on the *Human Right to Safe and Clean Drinking Water and Sanitation* (2008), UN Resolution 64/292 on the *Human right to Water and Sanitation* (2010) and UN Resolution 70/169 the *Right to Safe Drinking Water and Sanitation* (2015).

International environmental treaties are relevant to the matter of sustainable water use and management as well as protection of water and ecosystems. The *Ramsar Convention on Wetlands of International Importance* (1973) provides for the listing, protection and sustainable use of a wide range of wetland types (including permanent and temporary, running or still waters). The *Convention on the Protection and Use of Transboundary Watercourses and International Lakes* (1992) started as a European regional treaty and was opened up to all UN member states. It has attracted relatively few parties beyond Europe but does include relevant provisions on sustainable use of transboundary watercourses and addressing issues such as pollution. The *Protocol on Water and Health* (1999) under the convention provides a framework for quality drinking water including targets for quality, performance of wastewater treatment and waterborne disease management. The *UN Convention to Combat Desertification* (1994), for example, obliges state parties 'to promote cooperation in the fields of conservation of water resources' (Article 4), which is relevant to management and also transboundary water resources. Other international environmental law treaties (e.g., the *Convention on Biological Diversity* (1992)) seek to protect ecosystems including those found in or related to water. Yet despite all of these international law developments, sustainable water resource management and human health risks relating to water and lack of sanitation have not been addressed. SDG 6 goes beyond the international law summarised previously in setting quantitative and time-limited goals and bringing together the different legal sub-fields.[8]

International environmental law is also relevant to energy, particularly as there is no recognised body of 'international energy law'. The *UN Framework Convention on Climate Change* (1992) seeks to stabilise greenhouse gas emissions (Article 2), much of which is related to energy production, but does not mention renewables. The subsequent *Kyoto Protocol* (1997) set emissions reduction targets for developed nations but did not include any goals related to access to energy services. Nevertheless, the *Kyoto Protocol* did include a provision encouraging states 'to promote sustainable development' (Article 2). The *Paris Agreement* (2015) facilitates domestically led commitments through the requirement for each nation to submit a Nationally Determined

8 Joyeeta Gupta and Hilmer Bosch, 'SDG 6: Clean Water and Sanitation' in J Ebbsson and E Hey (eds), *The Cambridge Handbook of the Sustainable Development Goals and International Law* (Cambridge: Cambridge University Press, 2022) 177.

Contribution document which includes mitigation actions (Article 3) – some of which would include emission reductions in accordance with Article 6. The *Paris Agreement* also refers to financial flows that should support transitions to 'low greenhouse gas emissions and climate-resilient development' (Article 2(1)(c)). Multiple articles include reference to promoting and supporting sustainable development, although these are not binding.

International trade and investment laws are also relevant, as energy is a valuable commodity, as are energy efficient technologies. World Trade Organization (WTO) rules seek to ensure that trade is conducted without discrimination and prevent nations from discriminating between trading partners.[9] This can create barriers for more environmentally friendly goods and services, such as renewables, because a nation cannot prefer these over conventional energy products. The WTO allows only limited (and difficult to successfully apply) exceptions where certain products or services are necessary to protect human, animal or plant life or if they relate to the conservation of exhaustible natural resources.[10] The Doha round of negotiations (commencing in 2001) were aimed at reforming trade rules to better align WTO and environmental treaty rules, including removing barriers to environmental goods and services, but these have not been concluded.[11] Similarly, investment laws tend to favour economic goals over social and environmental ones.[12] Although there is no body of international energy law, there are some relevant agreements. The *Energy Charter Treaty* (1994) focuses on trade, energy efficiency and secure investments and requires member states to minimise harmful impacts from energy use (Article 19). The supporting *Protocol on Energy Efficiency and Related Environmental Aspects* (1998) requires states to develop policies to improve energy efficiency and reduce environmental impacts. Renewable energy is addressed in several instruments, including the *Convention on Nuclear Safety* (1994) and the non-binding the UN General Assembly Resolution on *Promotion of new and renewable sources of energy* (2012).

The international rules summarised previously demonstrate some measures that support SDGs 6 and 7 but also a number of conflicting norms.

4.3 SDG 6 – clean water and sanitation

Providing universal access to clean water and sanitation is a fundamental right and basic need and yet has remained an elusive goal. The targets in SDG 6

9 WTO, *Principles of the Trading System*, https://www.wto.org/english/thewto_e/whatis_e/tif_e/fact2_e.htm.

10 *General Agreement on Tariffs and Trade*, Article 20(b) and (g).

11 WTO, *The Doha Round*, https://www.wto.org/english/tratop_e/dda_e/dda_e.htm.

12 Stuart Bruce and Jorge E Viñuales, 'SDG7: Ensure Access to Affordable, Reliable, Sustainable and Modern Energy for All' in J Ebbesson and E Hey (eds), *The Cambridge Handbook of the Sustainable Development Goals and International Law* (Cambridge: Cambridge University Press, 2022) 202.

seek to advance the aim, and the following discussion is divided into access, quality, sustainable management and use and implementation measures.

Goal 6. Ensure availability and sustainable management of water and sanitation for all

Targets	*Indicators*
6.1 By 2030, achieve universal and equitable access to safe and affordable drinking water for all	*6.1.1 Proportion of population using safely managed drinking water services*
6.2 By 2030, achieve access to adequate and equitable sanitation and hygiene for all and end open defecation, paying special attention to the needs of women and girls and those in vulnerable situations	*6.2.1 Proportion of population using (a) safely managed sanitation services and (b) a hand-washing facility with soap and water*
6.3 By 2030, improve water quality by reducing pollution, eliminating dumping and minimizing release of hazardous chemicals and materials, halving the proportion of untreated wastewater and substantially increasing recycling and safe reuse globally	*6.3.1 Proportion of domestic and industrial wastewater flows safely treated* *6.3.2 Proportion of bodies of water with good ambient water quality*
6.4 By 2030, substantially increase water-use efficiency across all sectors and ensure sustainable withdrawals and supply of freshwater to address water scarcity and substantially reduce the number of people suffering from water scarcity	*6.4.1 Change in water-use efficiency over time* *6.4.2 Level of water stress: freshwater withdrawal as a proportion of available freshwater resources*
6.5 By 2030, implement integrated water resources management at all levels, including through transboundary cooperation as appropriate	*6.5.1 Degree of integrated water resources management* *6.5.2 Proportion of transboundary basin area with an operational arrangement for water cooperation*
6.6 By 2020, protect and restore water-related ecosystems, including mountains, forests, wetlands, rivers, aquifers and lakes	*6.6.1 Change in the extent of water-related ecosystems over time*
6.a By 2030, expand international cooperation and capacity-building support to developing countries in water- and sanitation-related activities and programmes, including water harvesting, desalination, water efficiency, wastewater treatment, recycling and reuse technologies	*6.a.1 Amount of water- and sanitation-related official development assistance that is part of a government coordinated spending plan*
6.b Support and strengthen the participation of local communities in improving water and sanitation management	*6.b.1 Proportion of local administrative units with established and operational policies and procedures for participation of local communities in water and sanitation management*

4.3.1 *Access*

The first two targets are focused on providing access to freshwater and sanitation for all by 2030 and therefore prioritise human health.[13] Target 6.1 is aimed at 'universal and equitable' access to 'safe and affordable' drinking water. The aim of Target 6.2, however, is 'adequate and equitable' sanitation and hygiene for all, paying special regard to women, girls and vulnerable people. The words safe and adequate relate to quality but do not necessarily require high quality. The affordability requirement for drinking water is not included for sanitation. The indicators for both targets measure the proportion of people with such access.

4.3.2 *Quality*

Target 6.3 is focused on improving water quality – water system health – regardless of whether it is used for drinking or sanitation. Indicator 6.3.1 relates to wastewater treatment and not the other aspects of the target. Indicator 6.3.2 measures bodies of water with 'good ambient quality', which addresses, in part, pollution, dumping and release of pollutants; no indicator addresses recycling and reuse.

4.3.3 *Sustainable management and use*

Target 6.4 seeks to increase water use efficiency across all sectors and reduce scarcity for all people. Indicator 6.4.1 measures changes in water use efficiency, and Indicator 6.4.2 measures levels of water stress as a simple ratio of withdrawal as proportion of available water resources – withdrawing more than 25 per cent of renewable freshwater equates to water stress.[14] Target 6.5 focuses on the application of integrated water resource management, although integration is hard to measure. This target also seeks to overcome issues managing bodies of water that cross national boundaries. Target 6.6 is about protection and restoration of water-related ecosystems, including bodies of water (wetlands, rivers, lakes and wetlands), as well as forests and mountains.

4.3.4 *Implementation measures*

Target 6.a is about top-down global cooperation and capacity building to support developing states and improve all aspects of water and sanitation. Indicator 6.a.1 only captures official development assistance. Target 6.b is focused on communities themselves and their participation in improving

13 Bruce and Viñuales (2022) 167.
14 Advocates for International Development, *SDG 6* (2022) 7.

water and sanitation management, with measures referring to policies for local participation.

4.4 SDG 7 – affordable and clean energy

A specific goal focused on energy was new in the SDGs, and SDG 7 supports increased access, improved efficiency and a shift to renewable sources. All four of the targets are to be achieved by 2030, but notably none are quantified. It has one of the smallest numbers of targets, which cover access, efficiency and renewable energy, each of which is explored in the section that follows.

Goal 7. Ensure access to affordable, reliable, sustainable and modern energy for all

Targets	*Indicators*
7.1 By 2030, ensure universal access to affordable, reliable and modern energy services	*7.1.1 Proportion of population with access to electricity* *7.1.2 Proportion of population with primary reliance on clean fuels and technology*
7.2 By 2030, increase substantially the share of renewable energy in the global energy mix	*7.2.1 Renewable energy share in the total final energy consumption*
7.3 By 2030, double the global rate of improvement in energy efficiency	*7.3.1 Energy intensity measured in terms of primary energy and GDP*
7.a By 2030, enhance international cooperation to facilitate access to clean energy research and technology, including renewable energy, energy efficiency and advanced and cleaner fossil-fuel technology, and promote investment in energy infrastructure and clean energy technology	*7.a.1 International financial flows to developing countries in support of clean energy research and development and renewable energy production, including in hybrid systems*
7.b By 2030, expand infrastructure and upgrade technology for supplying modern and sustainable energy services for all in developing countries, in particular least developed countries, small island developing States and landlocked developing countries, in accordance with their respective programmes of support	*7.b.1 Installed renewable energy-generating capacity in developing and developed countries (in watts per capita)*

4.4.1 Access

Target 7.1 seeks to ensure 'affordable, reliable and modern' energy to all. The word 'modern' is undefined, but the indicators suggest it relates to clean fuels and technology, which can include renewables but also cleaner fossil fuels that reduce pollution. Affordability is included, and yet no indicator specifically focuses on this aspect. Target 7.b relates to infrastructure and technology for 'modern and sustainable energy services'. Such services are vital if access is to be improved. It is the only target in SDG 7 mentioning sustainability and also refers explicitly to least developed nations and small island developing states.

4.4.2 Efficiency

Target 7.3 focuses on energy efficiency, with a goal to double it by 2030. Improving efficiency ought to lower the cumulative environmental impact of energy production, which is important as human populations grow. Both energy efficiency and transitions to renewable energy are needed if global goals are to be met.

4.4.3 Renewable energy

Target 7.2 focuses on increasing the proportion of energy produced from renewable resources. This aim should benefit those people dependent upon energy produced from fossil fuel imports and also deliver environmental benefits, provided that the mining of minerals needed (such as lithium, copper, nickel and rare earth minerals used in batteries) is undertaken sustainably. No quantified target is included, though, and 'increase substantially' is vague in comparison to others and especially so given global commitments to achieve net zero carbon emissions by 2030.[15] Target 7.a is about enabling energy transitions relating to renewable energy and efficiency through international cooperation and financial and technological support for developing nations. This target is similar to other capacity-building aims throughout the SDGs. Target 7.b relates to infrastructure and is the only target in SDG 7 mentioning sustainability.

4.5 Progressing SDGs 6 and 7

Social sustainability is one of the pillars of sustainable development, highlighting the significance of SDGs 6 and 7 that contribute to it. SDG 6 addresses access and use of freshwater but does not engage with the issue of property rights – ownership of water – nor climate impacts on freshwater. Energy, on the other hand, is recognised as a commodity, and affordability issues affect

15 UN, *Climate Action*, https://www.un.org/en/climatechange/net-zero-coalition.

many people in all parts of the world, yet no SDG 7 indicator specifically focuses on this aspect.

4.5.1 Linkages with other SDGs[16]

SDGs 1, 6 and 7 are inherently connected, as people living in poverty often do not have access to water and sanitation or affordable and reliable energy. Health and disease risks are exacerbated when there is poor access to freshwater and sanitation, and Targets 3.3 and 3.9 refer explicitly to water. Similarly, the health-related impacts of using polluting energies link SDGs 3 and 7. Women's water needs and uses are different to men's, and this implicates SDG 5, and household access to water and energy will enhance women's ability to undertake other activities. Water is essential to agriculture, and therefore sustainable water use management (and the success of SDG 6) will support food production (SDG 2). Water is also needed for energy production (SDG 7), and water and energy are essential for economic growth and productivity (SDG 8), as well as infrastructure and industrialisation (SDG 9). Both SDGs 6 and 7 include targets focused on developing nations, which contribute to SDG 10. Yet there are tensions here because problems with water quality and equitable access are caused by agriculture, industrialisation, urbanisation, population and economic growth and development more broadly. Therefore, SDGs which seek to expand activities in these areas could interfere with the achievement of SDG 6. Furthermore, industrialisation and economic growth – seen as essential for development – require energy, and its production (if not entirely from renewable resources) can have negative environmental impacts and undermine SDGs 13, 14 and 15, for example. Water-related disasters are singled out in Target 11.5 in the context of sustainable cities and settlements. Sustainable water management is critical for sustainable consumption and production (see Targets 12.2 and 12.4 in particular). Addressing climate change (SDG 13) is important to prevent impacts on freshwater resources and the conservation of ecosystems highlighted in SDG 6 and aligns well with SDGs 14 and 15 (life below water and on land). Reducing the production of energy from fossil fuels and transitioning to renewable energy are clearly needed to achieve SDG 13, and yet SDG 7 does not mention climate change (and SDG 13 does not refer to energy or power). Clean energy production is also relevant to sustainable consumption and production (SDG 12 – with Indicator 12.a.1 being identical to 7.b.1) and to protect life below water and on land which may be impacted by oil and gas production and mining (SDGs 13 and 14).

16 **For a broader examination of linkages with SDG 7, see International Council for Science,** *A Guide to SDG Interactions: From Science to Implementation* **(2017), https://council.science/wp-content/uploads/2017/05/SDGs-Guide-to-Interactions.pdf.**

4.5.2 The role of law and policy

Law is not explicitly mentioned in SDG 6, although policies and procedures feature in Indicator 6.b.1. Neither law nor policy are referred to in SDG 7 despite international law obligations referred to in Section 4.2. Nevertheless, water and natural resource law has a critical role to play in access (Target 6.1) and freshwater management (Targets 6.4, 6.b). Similarly, energy laws that mostly exist at the national level are critical to the achievement of all of the targets in SDG 7 and most particularly to progress the renewable energy transition. Environmental law is vital for pollution control (Target 6.3 for water and Indicator 7.1.1 on clean energy), as well as protecting and restoring water-related ecosystems (Target 6.6). Various fields of law (taxation, corporations and investment law) could support the development and/or expansion of wastewater management, recycling and reuse facilities, as well as energy efficiency and clean and renewable energy expansion. In particular, law and policy can catalyse action by setting efficiency and performance standards, as well as promoting investment in water and energy transitions.

4.6 Conclusion

Achieving SDGs 6 and 7 would significantly improve social sustainability and simultaneously advance environmental sustainability. Yet progress has slipped on SDG 6, with 50 per cent of the targets stagnating or regressing.[17] In relation to SDG 7, progress is better, with moderate or marginal progress on 60 per cent of the targets, but 20 per cent remain off track.[18] In 2023, the UN High Level Political Forum on Sustainable Development (HLPF) reaffirmed its 'resolve to realize our vision of a world with access to . . . safe drinking water, sanitation and hygiene, affordable, reliable, sustainable and modern energy'.[19] That resolve must be converted into action if SDGs 4 and 5 are to be achieved by 2030.

17 UNGA, *Progress Towards the Sustainable Development Goals* (2024), https://unstats.un.org/sdgs/files/report/2024/SG-SDG-Progress-Report-2024-advanced-unedited-version.pdf.

18 UNGA, *Progress Towards the Sustainable Development Goals* (2024). See also Our World in Data, *SDG Tracker: Measuring Progress Towards the Sustainable Development Goals* (2023), https://ourworldindata.org/sdgs.

19 UNGA, *Political Declaration of the High-Level Political Forum on Sustainable Development Convened Under the Auspices of the General Assembly* (2023), https://www.un.org/en/conferences/SDGSummit2023/political-declaration, para 18.

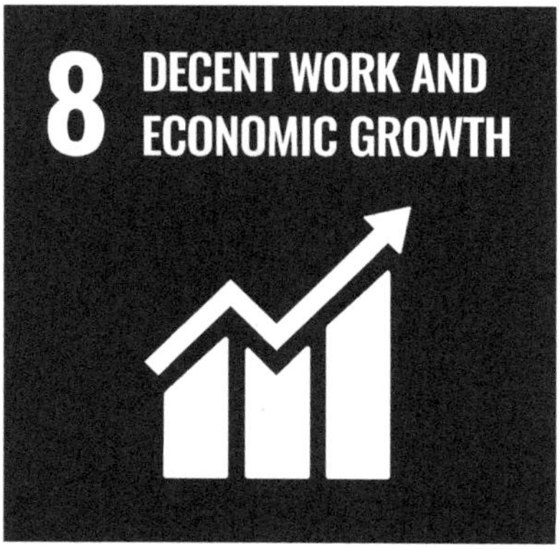
8
DECENT WORK AND
ECONOMIC GROWTH

9
INDUSTRY, INNOVATION
AND INFRASTRUCTURE

10
REDUCED
INEQUALITIES

Timeline of key developments in employment, economies and industrialisation

Soft Initiatives	*Date*	*Legally Binding Conventions*
International Labour Organization created	**1919**	ILO Constitution
	1930	ILO Convention No.29 on Forced Labour
ILO Declaration of Philadelphia	**1944**	
Universal Declaration of Human Rights	**1948**	ILO Convention No.87 on Freedom of Association and Protection of the Right to Organise
	1949	ILO Convention No.98 on the Right to Organise and Collective Bargaining Convention
	1951	ILO Convention No. 100: Equal Remuneration
	1957	ILO Convention No.105 on the Abolition of Forced Labour
	1958	ILO Convention No.111 on Concerning Discrimination in Respect of Employment and Occupation
	1965	International Convention on the Elimination of All Forms of Racial Discrimination
	1966	International Covenant on Economic, Social and Cultural Rights International Covenant on Civil and Political Rights
	1973	ILO Convention No.138 on the Minimum Age Convention
	1979	Convention on the Elimination of All Forms of Discrimination against Women
Declaration on the Right to Development	**1986**	
	1989	Convention on the Rights of the Child
	1990	International Convention on the Protection of the Rights of All Migrant Workers and Members of their Families
	1992	UN Framework Convention on Climate Change
	1994	Agreement on Trade-Related Aspects of Intellectual Property Rights (TRIPS Agreement)

(*Continued*)

(Continued)

Soft Initiatives	*Date*	*Legally Binding Conventions*
World Trade Organization (WTO) founded	**1995**	
	1997	Kyoto Protocol
ILO Declaration on Fundamental Principles and Rights at Work	**1998**	
	1999	ILO Convention No.182: Worst Forms of Child Labour
UN Global Compact Principles	**2000**	
Equator Principles	**2003**	
	2006	Convention on the Rights of Persons with Disabilities
UN Declaration of the Rights of Indigenous Peoples WTO Enhanced Integrated Frame-work for Trade-related Technical Assistance to Least Developed Countries	**2007**	
ILO Declaration on Social Justice for a Fair Globalization	**2008**	
ILO Global Jobs Pact	**2009**	
UN Guiding Principles on Business and Human Rights	**2011**	
Lima Declaration Towards inclusive and sustainable industrial development	**2013**	
	2014	Protocol to the 1930 ILO Convention on Forced Labour
Agenda 2030 and the SDGs Addis Ababa Action Agenda ILO Guidelines on Just Transitions	**2015**	Paris Agreement
UN Global Compact for Safe, Orderly and Regular Migration	**2018**	
ILO Centenary Declaration for the Future of Work ILO Future of Work Initiative	**2019**	

5 Employment, economies and industrialisation

SDGs 8, 9 and 10

5.1 Background

The United Nations (UN) Charter (1945) formally recognised the entitlement of states to equal treatment through the 'principle of sovereign equality' (Article 2). Nevertheless, it is clear that entrenched inequalities exist between nations, particularly with regard to economic and developmental status.[1] Over 1 billion people live in least developed nations, where dependence on the export of commodities together with debt burdens were worsening in 2015 and have deteriorated since.[2] In addition, the least developed nations' environments are affected by the economic activities of developed states and continue to be impacted more severely by trade restrictions and rising food prices.[3] In contrast, the most innovative economies in the world, and those with the most advanced technology, are all in developed nations.[4] There is little doubt that inequity and inequality between nations persist and jeopardise progress towards sustainable development. Industrialisation is a way for developing countries to progress, but there is a risk of unintended consequences, as economic growth often risks environmental degradation and loss of cultural diversity.

The Millennium Development Goals (MDGs) included several relevant targets, but the ongoing need to address inequality led to *Agenda 2030* including state commitments to creating 'conditions for sustainable, inclusive and sustained economic growth, shared prosperity and decent work for all, taking into account different levels of national development and capacities'.[5]

1 UN, *Country Classification* https://www.un.org/en/development/desa/policy/wesp/wesp_current/2014wesp_country_classification.pdf.

2 UNCTAD, *Key Statistics on LDCs*, https://unctad.org/topic/least-developed-countries/chart-of-the-month.

3 UNCTAD, *Food Export Restrictions Hurt Millions in Least Developed Countries,* https://unctad.org/topic/least-developed-countries/chart-march-to-june-2022.

4 WIPO, *Global Innovation Index*, https://www.wipo.int/web/global-innovation-index.

5 UNGA, *Transforming Our World: The 2030 Agenda for Sustainable Development* (2015), para 3.

DOI: 10.4324/9781003583981-5

Agenda 2030 tends to put a positive (and arguably utopian) spin on the role of industrialisation and economic growth by including the aim 'to ensure that all human beings can enjoy prosperous and fulfilling lives and that economic, social and technological progress occurs in harmony with nature'.[6] Trade-offs do exist, and in some respects the Sustainable Development Goals (SDGs) seek to address them. SDG 9 recognises the central role that infrastructure plays in economies and the need for industrialisation to be sustainable and inclusive. Decent work for all in SDG 8, for example, focuses on overcoming inequalities in the context of employment, with constraints on economic growth in order to balance developmental and social sustainability. These goals are relevant to reducing inequalities (SDG 10), yet more systemic action is needed to ensure fairness, drive necessary trade and investment and catalyse global cooperation.

This chapter explores SDGs 8, 9 and 10 together, as, in part, they are all essential for sustainable development but also risk being disconnected from other social and environmental goals because of their economic and developmental core. The chapter commences by explaining the international legal backdrop to these goals before examining the detail of the SDGs, targets and indicators and how we can progress them.

5.2 The international law and policy context

The SDGs considered in this chapter are not clearly linked with any single body of international law and instead are supported by human rights, labour, trade, investment and economic law. The International Labour Organization (ILO) was formed in 1919, well before the UN, and has taken the lead in setting labour standards which many nations have embedded in domestic law and policy. From the outset, the ILO argued that 'labour is not a commodity' and that economic policies should be based on 'social justice'.[7] Early instruments included the *ILO Convention on Forced Labour* (1930) and the *ILO Convention no. 87 on Freedom of Association and Protection of the Right to Organise* (1948), which confirmed industrial action as a legitimate activity of workers. Core labour standards were set out in the 1998 *Declaration of Fundamental Principles and Rights at Work* and included prohibitions on key matters such as forced and child labour as well as discrimination. 'Decent work' – which features in both *Agenda 2030* and the SDGs – is defined by the ILO as including four strategic objectives: promoting employment, developing and enhancing social protection, promoting social dialogue and tripartism and recognising fundamental principles and rights at work.[8] In 2019 the

6 *Agenda 2030*, Preamble, under the banner of 'Prosperity'.
7 See *ILO Declaration of Philadelphia* (1944), Articles I(a) and II.
8 *Declaration on Social Justice for a Fair Globalization* (2008), Article I(A).

ILO Centenary Declaration reaffirmed workers' rights to fundamental protections, an adequate minimum wage, maximum time limits on working hours and safety and health at work (Article III(B)). The declaration also supported advancing youth employment and women's economic empowerment, both of which link directly to SDG 8.

Simultaneously, international human rights law supported rights at work. The *International Covenant on Civil and Political Rights* (1966) (ICCPR) prohibits slavery and forced and compulsory labour, (Article 8) and confirms the right to freedom of association, 'including the right to form and join trade unions' (Article 22). The *International Covenant on Economic, Social and Cultural Rights* (1966) (ICESCR) recognises the right to work and the right to the opportunity to gain a living from work (Article 6), as well as the right 'to the enjoyment of just and favourable conditions of work' (Article 7). In addition, the *Protocol of 2014 to the Forced Labour Convention* added to existing protections, particularly with respect to slavery-like practices such as modern slavery.

Underpinning economic growth, industrialisation and innovation is international trade and investment law. Although much of the law that supports economic growth was developed largely in isolation of socio-environmental concerns, more recently trade and investment agreements have recognised the need to protect the environment and some socio-cultural rights. The United Nations Conference on Trade and Development (UNCTAD) was established in 1964 to address the challenges facing developing nations in the context of international trade. Yet the World Trade Organization (WTO) supports equality by applying the same rules to all nations regardless of how ill equipped developing countries may be to compete in global markets. International trade law has incorporated some exceptions including 'special and differential treatment provisions' that allow developing countries to be given more favourable treatment than other nations.[9] Differential treatment also appears in international environmental law via the principle of 'common but differentiated responsibilities', which recognises that all nations are responsible for addressing global environmental problems but not equally so.[10] This has allowed for differential treatment through, for example, extended timeframes for developing nations to implement obligations and/or tailored quantified limits to achieve collective action on shared global challenges.[11] The WTO has also agreed to other differential measures, including that it will not impose

9 WTO, *Special and Differential Treatment Provisions,* https://www.wto.org/english/tratop_e/devel_e/dev_special_differential_provisions_e.htm.

10 The principle was articulated in the *Rio Declaration* (Principle 7) and formalised in the *UN Framework Convention on Climate Change* (Articles 3 and 4).

11 See, for example, the *Montreal Protocol on Substances that Deplete the Ozone Layer* (1987), which provided differential treatment for developing nations: UNEP, *About Montreal Protocol*, https://www.unep.org/ozonaction/who-we-are/about-montreal-protocol.

conditions on trade relating to labour standards.[12] This means that states can impose trade restrictions under the General Exceptions clauses of *General Agreement on Tariffs and Trade* (GATT) and the *General Agreement on Trade in Services* (GATS) for failure to adhere to labour standards. The WTO has recently adopted the *Enhanced Integrated Framework* (2019), a partnership dedicated to assisting least-developed countries to use trade for growth, sustainable development and poverty reduction.[13] International investment law also supports growth, yet tensions arise when investment agreements seek to restrict the host state's ability to regulate worker rights on the basis that improved labour standards reduce the value of the investment.[14] Nevertheless, more recent investment agreements do the reverse and restrict the host state's reduction in labour standards.[15]

Innovation does not feature strongly in international law, although some regimes support technology transfer (such as the *Convention on Biological Diversity* (CBD), *UN Framework Convention on Climate Change* and the *UN Convention on the Law of the Sea*) in the context of environmental objectives rather than developmental goals. The CBD similarly includes reference to intellectual property (IP) law. IP laws are relevant for innovation, as they provide exclusive rights (copyright, patent, trademark, etc.) to innovators. The *Agreement on Trade-Related Aspects of Intellectual Property Rights* (TRIPS Agreement) (1994) sets minimum standards for IP protection and also includes some differential measures, such as longer time periods, that might assist developing nations.[16]

As this short summary indicates, there are international laws that seek to address inequality at the individual level within nations. Whilst some international agreements allow for differential measures between nations, there is no global regime focused on overcoming inequality between nations. It is against this backdrop that SDGs 8, 9 and 10 are explored.

5.3 SDG 8 – decent work and economic growth

Economic growth is seen as a way to address poverty and facilitate development, and yet its unfettered pursuit can undermine the provision of 'decent

12 Tonia Novitz, 'SDG 8: Promote Sustained, Inclusive and Sustainable Economic Growth, Full and Productive Employment and Decent Work for All' in J Ebbesson and E Hey (eds), *The Cambridge Handbook of the Sustainable Development Goals and International Law* (Cambridge: CUP, 2022) 220.

13 EIF, https://www.enhancedif.org/.

14 Novitz (2022) 222.

15 See, for example, *Agreement Between the Government of Hungary and the Government of the Republic of Cabo Verde for the Promotion and Reciprocal Protection of Investments* (Cape Verde, Hungary: BIT, 2019), Article 2(8).

16 WTO, *Overview: The TRIPS Agreement,* https://www.wto.org/english/tratop_e/trips_e/intel2_e.htm.

work for all'. By combining these two elements in one SDG and making strong references to ILO labour standards, SDG 8 seeks to balance economic and social aims. This SDG can be divided into those targets seeking to enhance economic growth, provide employment, protect workers and facilitate SDG 8.

Goal 8. Promote sustained, inclusive and sustainable economic growth, full and productive employment and decent work for all

Targets	*Indicators*
8.1 Sustain per capita economic growth in accordance with national circumstances and, in particular, at least 7 per cent gross domestic product growth per annum in the least developed countries	*8.1.1 Annual growth rate of real GDP per capita*
8.2 Achieve higher levels of economic productivity through diversification, technological upgrading and innovation, including through a focus on high-value added and labour-intensive sectors	*8.2.1 Annual growth rate of real GDP per employed person*
8.3 Promote development-oriented policies that support productive activities, decent job creation, entrepreneurship, creativity and innovation, and encourage the formalization and growth of micro-, small- and medium-sized enterprises, including through access to financial services	*8.3.1 Proportion of informal employment in total employment, by sector and sex*
8.4 Improve progressively, through 2030, global resource efficiency in consumption and production and endeavour to decouple economic growth from environmental degradation, in accordance with the 10-Year Framework of Programmes on Sustainable Consumption and Production, with developed countries taking the lead	*8.4.1 Material footprint, material footprint per capita, and material footprint per GDP* *8.4.2 Domestic material consumption, domestic material consumption per capita, and domestic material consumption per GDP*
8.5 By 2030, achieve full and productive employment and decent work for all women and men, including for young people and persons with disabilities, and equal pay for work of equal value	*8.5.1 Average hourly earnings of employees, by sex, age, occupation and persons with disabilities* *8.5.2 Unemployment rate, by sex, age and persons with disabilities*
8.6 By 2020, substantially reduce the proportion of youth not in employment, education or training	*8.6.1 Proportion of youth (aged 15–24 years) not in education, employment or training*

(*Continued*)

(Continued)

Targets	*Indicators*
8.7 Take immediate and effective measures to eradicate forced labour, end modern slavery and human trafficking and secure the prohibition and elimination of the worst forms of child labour, including recruitment and use of child soldiers, and by 2025 end child labour in all its forms	*8.7.1 Proportion and number of children aged 5–17 years engaged in child labour, by sex and age*
8.8 Protect labour rights and promote safe and secure working environments for all workers, including migrant workers, in particular women migrants, and those in precarious employment	*8.8.1 Fatal and non-fatal occupational injuries per 100,000 workers, by sex and migrant status* *8.8.2 Level of national compliance with labour rights (freedom of association and collective bargaining) based on International Labour Organization (ILO) textual sources and national legislation, by sex and migrant status*
8.9 By 2030, devise and implement policies to promote sustainable tourism that creates jobs and promotes local culture and products	*8.9.1 Tourism direct GDP as a proportion of total GDP and in growth rate*
8.10 Strengthen the capacity of domestic financial institutions to encourage and expand access to banking, insurance and financial services for all	*8.10.1 (a) Number of commercial bank branches per 100,000 adults and (b) number of automated teller machines (ATMs) per 100,000 adults* *8.10.2 Proportion of adults (15 years and older) with an account at a bank or other financial institution or with a mobile-money-service provider*
8.a Increase Aid for Trade support for developing countries, in particular least developed countries, including through the Enhanced Integrated Framework for Trade-related Technical Assistance to Least Developed Countries	*8.a.1 Aid for Trade commitments and disbursements*
8.b By 2020, develop and operationalize a global strategy for youth employment and implement the Global Jobs Pact of the International Labour Organization	*8.b.1 Existence of a developed and operationalized national strategy for youth employment, as a distinct strategy or as part of a national employment strategy*

5.3.1 Economic growth

Target 8.1 is squarely focused on sustained economic growth measured in terms of GDP per capita with a quantified minimum goal for least developed countries. Targets 8.2 and 8.3 seek to improve productivity with the goal of increasing high-value-added labour output and promoting policies that support access to financial services, which could enable a more diverse mix of enterprises and economic activities. Target 8.4 is about efficient use of global resources to decouple economic growth from environmental damage, measured in terms of footprint and domestic material consumption. Although the headline goal is 'sustained, inclusive and sustainable economic growth', the word 'sustain' appears only once. None of these targets is time limited.

5.3.2 Employment

Targets 8.5 and 8.6 focus on 'full and productive' employment with 'decent work' and equal pay for all. Ensuring decent work is often linked to income inequalities but also workplace safety given that many people continue to work in dangerous conditions.[17] Target 8.9 requires states to devise and implement policies on sustainable tourism as a particular sector that is singled out. The focus of Target 8.6 is youth unemployment, education and training, with the indicator measuring those people between 15 and 24 years not engaged in one of these three areas. Youth are mentioned again in Target 8.b in the context of the ILO *Global Jobs Pact*.

5.3.3 Worker rights

Target 8.7 is about ending forced labour, modern slavery and human trafficking, yet the indicator only focuses on child labour. Labour rights and safe work environments are the focus on Target 8.8. Indicator 8.8.1 measures injuries as a proxy for safe work, and 8.8.2 assesses compliance with ILO agreements referred to in Section 5.2.

5.3.4 Facilitating measures

Target 8.10 requires states to build 'the capacity of financial service institutions' in order to facilitate services needed for growth and employment. The indicators focus on number of banks and ATMs and the proportion of adults with an account. Target 8.a refers explicitly to increasing aid for trade through the *Enhanced Integrated Framework for Trade-related Technical Assistance to Least Developed Countries*, and Target 8.b supports the *Global Jobs Pact*, both of which are outlined in Section 5.2.

17 Novitz (2022) 209.

5.4 SDG 9 – industry, innovation and infrastructure

Quality and reliable infrastructure and capabilities are a foundation for industrialisation and innovation. In turn, increasing infrastructure and industrialisation are measures of development themselves and must be done sustainably if the SDGs are to be achieved. A review of SDG 9 demonstrates efforts made to balance the tensions between growth and industrialisation and ensuring equity and inclusion. The following discussion is divided into groupings of targets on infrastructure, industrialisation and capacity building.

Goal 9. Build resilient infrastructure, promote inclusive and sustainable industrialization and foster innovation

Targets	*Indicators*
9.1 Develop quality, reliable, sustainable and resilient infrastructure, including regional and transborder infrastructure, to support economic development and human well-being, with a focus on affordable and equitable access for all	*9.1.1 Proportion of the rural population who live within 2 km of an all-season road* *9.1.2 Passenger and freight volumes, by mode of transport*
9.2 Promote inclusive and sustainable industrialization and, by 2030, significantly raise industry's share of employment and gross domestic product, in line with national circumstances, and double its share in least developed countries	*9.2.1 Manufacturing value added as a proportion of GDP and per capita* *9.2.2 Manufacturing employment as a proportion of total employment*
9.3 Increase the access of small-scale industrial and other enterprises, in particular in developing countries, to financial services, including affordable credit, and their integration into value chains and markets	*9.3.1 Proportion of small-scale industries in total industry value added* *9.3.2 Proportion of small-scale industries with a loan or line of credit*
9.4 By 2030, upgrade infrastructure and retrofit industries to make them sustainable, with increased resource-use efficiency and greater adoption of clean and environmentally sound technologies and industrial processes, with all countries taking action in accordance with their respective capabilities	*9.4.1 CO2 emission per unit of value added*
9.5 Enhance scientific research, upgrade the technological capabilities of industrial sectors in all countries, in particular developing countries, including, by 2030, encouraging innovation and substantially increasing the number of research and development workers per 1 million people and public and private research and development spending	*9.5.1 Research and development expenditure as a proportion of GDP* *9.5.2 Researchers (in full-time equivalent) per million inhabitants*

(*Continued*)

(Continued)

Targets	*Indicators*
9.a Facilitate sustainable and resilient infrastructure development in developing countries through enhanced financial, technological and technical support to African countries, least developed countries, landlocked developing countries and small island developing States	*9.a.1 Total official international support (official development assistance plus other official flows) to infrastructure*
9.b Support domestic technology development, research and innovation in developing countries, including by ensuring a conducive policy environment for, inter alia, industrial diversification and value addition to commodities	*9.b.1 Proportion of medium and high-tech industry value added in total value added*
9.c Significantly increase access to information and communications technology and strive to provide universal and affordable access to the Internet in least developed countries by 2020	*9.c.1 Proportion of population covered by a mobile network, by technology*

5.4.1 Infrastructure

Building infrastructure is needed to facilitate sustainable development, and Target 9.1 is focused on this aim and making such infrastructure affordable and equitable for all. This target is measured with reference to the availability of all-season roads (Indicator 9.1.1) and volumes of transport (Indicator 9.1.2). Upgrading existing infrastructure to make it sustainable is addressed in Target 9.4. Reference is made to 'clean' and 'environmentally sound technologies', and yet Indicator 9.4.1 measures only CO_2 emissions. Target 9.a seeks to facilitate 'sustainable and resilient infrastructure development' through increased support (financial and technical), particularly for vulnerable states.

5.4.2 Industrialisation

Manufacturing value added to GDP and related employment are the measures used to assess progress towards 'inclusive and sustainable industrialization' (Target 9.2). In addition to this, the proportion of small-scale industries and the finance available to them is promoted by Target 9.3, which ought to contribute to social sustainability by supporting local livelihoods.

5.4.3 Capacity building

Enhancing scientific research and technological capabilities will be needed to advance industrialisation and development, and Target 9.5 seeks to achieve this and to encourage innovation. The indicators include both expenditure and researchers engaged. This aim is complemented by Target 9.b, which is about supporting development, research and innovation in developing countries with specific reference to policy for industrial diversification and value added commodities. The final target (9.c), as with several other SDGs, measures the proportion of the population covered by a mobile phone service as a measure of access to information and communication technologies.

5.5 SDG 10 – reduced inequalities

At the heart of *Agenda 2030* is the goal to 'leave no one behind', and reducing inequalities within and between nations is critical to that aim. SDG 10, though, focuses heavily on economic, trade and financial matters. The targets in this SDG are linked to income, empowerment and global trade and finance, and these three areas are explored in the following sections.

Goal 10. Reduce inequality within and among countries

Targets	*Indicators*
10.1 By 2030, progressively achieve and sustain income growth of the bottom 40 per cent of the population at a rate higher than the national average	*10.1.1 Growth rates of household expenditure or income per capita among the bottom 40 per cent of the population and the total population*
10.2 By 2030, empower and promote the social, economic and political inclusion of all, irrespective of age, sex, disability, race, ethnicity, origin, religion or economic or other status	*10.2.1 Proportion of people living below 50 per cent of median income, by sex, age and persons with disabilities*
10.3 Ensure equal opportunity and reduce inequalities of outcome, including by eliminating discriminatory laws, policies and practices and promoting appropriate legislation, policies and action in this regard	*10.3.1 Proportion of population reporting having personally felt discriminated against or harassed in the previous 12 months on the basis of a ground of discrimination prohibited under international human rights law*
10.4 Adopt policies, especially fiscal, wage and social protection policies, and progressively achieve greater equality	*10.4.1 Labour share of GDP* *10.4.2 Redistributive impact of fiscal policy*
10.5 Improve the regulation and monitoring of global financial markets and institutions and strengthen the implementation of such regulations	*10.5.1 Financial Soundness Indicators*

(*Continued*)

(Continued)

Targets	*Indicators*
10.6 Ensure enhanced representation and voice for developing countries in decision-making in global international economic and financial institutions in order to deliver more effective, credible, accountable and legitimate institutions	*10.6.1 Proportion of members and voting rights of developing countries in international organizations*
10.7 Facilitate orderly, safe, regular and responsible migration and mobility of people, including through the implementation of planned and well-managed migration policies	*10.7.1 Recruitment cost borne by employee as a proportion of monthly income earned in country of destination* *10.7.2 Proportion of countries with migration policies that facilitate orderly, safe, regular and responsible migration and mobility of people* *10.7.3 Number of people who died or disappeared in the process of migration towards an international destination* *10.7.4 Proportion of the population who are refugees, by country of origin*
10.a Implement the principle of special and differential treatment for developing countries, in particular least developed countries, in accordance with World Trade Organization agreements	*10.a.1 Proportion of tariff lines applied to imports from least developed countries and developing countries with zero-tariff*
10.b Encourage official development assistance and financial flows, including foreign direct investment, to States where the need is greatest, in particular least developed countries, African countries, small island developing States and landlocked developing countries, in accordance with their national plans and programmes	*10.b.1 Total resource flows for development, by recipient and donor countries and type of flow (e.g., official development assistance, foreign direct investment and other flows)*
10.c By 2030, reduce to less than 3 per cent the transaction costs of migrant remittances and eliminate remittance corridors with costs higher than 5 per cent	*10.c.1 Remittance costs as a proportion of the amount remitted*

5.5.1 Income

To facilitate equality within nations, Target 10.1 focuses on income growth of lower income earners at rates greater than the average. It does not, however, address overall income inequality between low income and top earners, which can still persist if the target is met.[18] Target 10.4 requires states to adopt fiscal, wage and social protection policies to better redistribute fiscal flows.

5.5.2 Empowerment

Target 10.2 seeks to empower all people, everywhere, through social, economic and political inclusion without discrimination. The indicator does not match the ambition of the target, as it does not measure the proportion of the population by race, ethnicity, origin or religion (10.2.1). However, Target 10.3 is focused more broadly on ensuring equal opportunity and eliminating discrimination, presumably within nations. Indicator 10.3.1 is the same as 16.b.1. Both of these targets align with human rights law and efforts to eliminate discrimination. Target 10.6 is about empowering developing nations to contribute to decision-making in global economic and financial institutions. Target 10.7 is also about a form of empowerment – the safe and responsible migration and mobility of peoples – although it has been noted that refugees are not mentioned.[19]

5.5.3 Global trade and finance

Target 10.5 is focused on global financial markets and ensuring nations implement international rules, whereas Target 10.a seeks to ensure implementation of global trade rules relating to the principles of special and differential treatment but does not mention other similar provisions outlined in Sections 5.2 and 10.c. Target 10.b encourages official development assistance for vulnerable nations to reduce the transaction costs of remittances[20] that reduce inequality.

5.6 Progressing SDGs 8, 9 and 10

SDGs 8, 9 and 10 are all at the interface of development and social aspects of sustainable development, with some connections to environmental

18 Philippe Cullet, 'SDG 10: Reduce Inequality Within and Among Countries' in J Ebbesson and E Hey (eds), *The Cambridge Handbook of The Sustainable Development Goals and International Law* (Cambridge: Cambridge University Press, 2022) 261.

19 Cullet (2022) 262.

20 Remittances are monies earned by migrants working in developed countries and sent back to their families living in developing nations.

sustainability. Clearly there is strong interconnectedness between these three SDGs as well as linkages with other goals. Synergies between goals will need to be harnessed, and tensions overcome, if significant progress is to be made by 2030. There is also an important role for law and policy to play, despite limited explicit references to these tools in the targets and indicators.

5.6.1 Linkages with other SDGs

Perhaps more than those discussed in any other chapter in this book, there are strong interactions between SDGs 8, 9 and 10 and other goals. Employment and the targets in SDGs 8 and 9 have both synergies and tensions with SDG 1 (end poverty), SDG 10 (inequality), and those goals focused on raising living standards, justice and social sustainability. Prospects for employment, for example, are enhanced where people have good health and quality education (SDGs 3 and 4). Target 8.4 relates to efficient use of global resources to achieve consumption and production, and the achievement of SDG 8 must be achieved taking into account the aims of SDG 7 (affordable and clean energy) and SDG 12 (sustainable consumption and production – with several identical indicators (8.4.1/12.2.1 and 8.4.2/12.2.2)) as well as SDGs 13 and 14 (life below water and on land). The SDG 8 focus on decent work with equal pay for all, and eradication of forced labour, modern slavery and human trafficking, link with SDG 5 and 15. SDG 16, and its target on inclusive decision-making (Target 16.7) applies to workplaces as well as other organisations. Target 8.6, on youth employment and education, has strong links with SDG 4. Those targets within SDG 10 related to empowerment link with human rights law and several other goals, including SDG 4. SDG 9 targets relating to innovation are supported by those focused on technology transfer in SDGs 14 and 17. SDG 9 and its focus on economic growth is, however, potentially conflict with the environmental sustainability goals (SDGs 12, 13 and 14). Similarly, achieving decent work for all (SDG 8) will be costly and therefore is in tension with economic growth (SDG 9). SDG 10 is inherently linked to SDG 5, which is the other goal focused on equality. SDG 10 is also closely connected with SDG 1, as it seeks to lift wages and therefore helps to address poverty. SDGs 2, 3, 6 and 7 are supported by SDG 10 as inequalities between nations exacerbate food insecurity, undermine health and well-being goals and hamper access to water and energy for all. Finally, SDGs 3, 4, 6, 7, 8, 9, 10, 12, 13, 14, 15, 16 and 17 all include specific goals focused on developing, least developed or vulnerable nations and therefore aim, at least in part, to address inequalities between nations (SDG 10).

5.6.2 The role of law and policy

SDGs 8, 9 and 10 make only limited reference to law and policy. SDG 8 includes an indicator that measures legislation supporting labour rights (Indicator 8.8.2). SDG 10 supports the elimination of discriminatory laws (Target

10.3 and Indicator 10.3.1 refer explicitly to international human rights law). Target 10.a makes specific reference to WTO agreements and the implementation of special and differential treatment. SDG 10 also refers to policy in Target 10.3 as well as 10.4 (policies to achieve greater equality) and 10.7 (migration policies). SDG 8 seeks to promote policies that are development oriented (Target 8.3) and focused on sustainable tourism (Target 8.9). SDG 9 encourages a conducive policy environment for technology development and innovation (Target 9.b).

It is clear that international human rights and labour law are important in eradicating forced labour, modern slavery and human trafficking, as well as addressing discrimination and securing labour rights (SDG 8) and protecting migrants and mobility (SDG 10). International trade, investment and intellectual property law are relevant to innovation and industrialisation (SDG 9). All of these sub-fields of law will be relevant to addressing inequality (SDG 10) as well as environmental, natural resources, land use and planning laws for tourism (SDG 8).

5.7 Conclusion

SDGs 8, 9 and 10 are vital in and of themselves and also for the success of other SDGs. The risk is that trade-offs will trump the synergies between developmental, social and environmental goals. Whether international law and the global systems that it supports are equipped to balance these tensions remains to be seen with divisions and tensions between trade/investment/economic law and environmental/human rights law. Progress on the SDGs indicates that there is much work to do, with SDGs 8 and 10 falling significantly behind, and only 30 per cent of SDG 9 is currently on track.[21] Furthermore, the UN High Level Political Forum on Sustainable Development (HLPF) noted in 2023 that there exists 'increased inequality exacerbated by weakened international solidarity and a shortfall of trust to jointly overcome these crises'.[22] In that context the HLPF committed to 'bold, ambitious, accelerated, just and transformative actions',[23] and these will surely be needed if the SDGs are to be met by 2030.

21 UNGA, *Progress Towards the Sustainable Development Goals* (2024), https://unstats.un.org/sdgs/files/report/2024/SG-SDG-Progress-Report-2024-advanced-unedited-version.pdf. See also Our World in Data, *SDG Tracker: Measuring Progress Towards the Sustainable Development Goals* (2023), https://ourworldindata.org/sdgs.

22 UNGA, *Political Declaration of the High-Level Political Forum on Sustainable Development Convened Under the Auspices of the General Assembly* (2023), https://www.un.org/en/conferences/SDGSummit2023/political-declaration, para 8.

23 UNGA, *Political Declaration of the High-Level Political Forum on Sustainable Development Convened Under the Auspices of the General Assembly* (2023), para 9.

Timeline of key developments in cities, settlements, consumption and production

Non-Binding Actions	*Date*	*Binding International Law*
Universal Declaration of Human Rights	**1948**	
UN Long-range International Programme of Concerted Action in the Field of Housing and related Facilities	**1959**	
	1966	International Covenant on Civil and Political Rights International Covenant on Economic, Social and Cultural Rights
Stockholm Declaration	**1972**	World Heritage Convention

(*Continued*)

(Continued)

Non-Binding Actions	*Date*	*Binding International Law*
UN-Habitat established	**1975**	
UN Conference on Human Settlements	**1976**	
	1979	Convention on the Elimination of All Forms of Discrimination Against Women
FAO International Code of Conduct on the Distribution and Use of Pesticides	**1985**	Vienna Convention for the Protection of the Ozone Layer
	1987	Montreal Protocol on Substances that Deplete the Ozone Layer
	1989	Basel Convention on the Control of Transboundary Movements of Hazardous Wastes and Their Disposal UN Convention on the Rights of the Child
International Decade for Natural Disaster Reduction	**1990**	
Rio Declaration	**1992**	
	1994	WTO Agreements UN Convention to Combat Desertification
	1998	Rotterdam Convention on the Prior Informed Consent Procedure for Certain Hazardous Chemicals and Pesticides in International Trade
	2001	Stockholm Convention on Persistent Organic Pollutants
UNESCO International Coalition of Inclusive and Sustainable Cities UNESCO Creative Cities Network	**2004**	
	2006	Convention on the Rights of Persons with Disabilities
UN Guiding Principles on Business and Human Rights	**2011**	
10 Year Framework of Programmes on Sustainable Consumption and Production Patterns (10YFP)	**2014**	
Sendai Framework on Disaster Risk Reduction 2015-2030	**2015**	Paris Agreement
New Urban Agenda	**2016**	
UNESCO Cities Platform	**2019**	
Second Decade of Action for Road Safety	**2021**	
UNEP Intergovernmental Negotiating Committee to develop a plastic pollution treaty	**2022**	

6 Cities, settlements, consumption and production

SDGs 11 and 12

6.1 Background

Urban areas are home to more than half of the world's population,[1] yet cities occupy 2 per cent of total land.[2] It was estimated in 2020 that 44 per cent of the world's population were living in cities and an additional 43 per cent in towns and urban areas, leaving only 13 per cent in rural places.[3] Cities are home to concentrations of wealth, productive activity and educational institutions that can contribute to the achievement of sustainable development, but they are also 'disproportionate contributors to global ecological dysfunction'.[4]

Cities and settlements benefited considerably from government action during the environmental movement of the 1970s, when air, water and land pollution reached crisis points.[5] The Brundtland Report (1987), *Our Common Future* devoted a whole chapter to 'The Urban Challenge'.[6] By 1992 it became clear that 'well planned and developed . . . cities can promote economically, socially and environmentally sustainable societies' and 'a holistic approach to urban development and human settlements that provides for affordable housing and infrastructure and prioritizes slum upgrading and urban

1 UN SDGs, *Goal 11: Make Cities Inclusive, Safe, Resilient and Sustainable*, https://www.un.org/sustainabledevelopment/cities/.

2 UN Habitat, *The New Urban Agenda*, https://habitat3.org/the-new-urban-agenda/.

3 Our World in Data, *Urbanization*, https://ourworldindata.org/urbanization.

4 Anél du Plessis, 'SDG 11: Make Cities and Human Settlements Inclusive, Safe, Resilient and Sustainable' in J Ebbesson and E Hey, *The Cambridge Handbook of The Sustainable Development Goals and International Law* (Cambridge: Cambridge University Press, 2022) 285.

5 See, for example, Australia's Select Committees on Air Pollution and Water Pollution 1968–70 http://navigatesenatecommittees.senate.gov.au/events/select-committees-on-air-pollution-and-water-pollution/62; Environment America, *From Earth Day 1970 to 2022: A Story of Progress*, https://environmentamerica.org/center/articles/earth-day-1970-2022-story-progress/.

6 See Chapter 1 for further discussion of the report. UNGA, *Report of the World Commission on Environment and Development, Our Common Future* (1987), https://sustainabledevelopment.un.org/content/documents/5987our-common-future.pdf.

DOI: 10.4324/9781003583981-6

regeneration'.[7] None of the Millennium Development Goals (MDGs) mentioned cites, and only Target 7.D refers to improving 'the lives of 100 million slum dwellers'.[8] *Agenda 2030* recognised 'that sustainable urban development and management are crucial to the quality of life of our people' (para 34) and included SDG 11 as one of the 17 goals.

The large human population in cities means that consumption is at their heart. Unsustainable consumption and production are arguably the root cause of the global problems we now face and were recognised as essential for sustainable development at the UN Conference on Environment and Development (1992).[9] As earlier chapters have shown, unnecessary waste combined with the drive for greater quantities of cheaper goods and services has led to negative human impacts and environmental degradation. Yet no MDG specifically focused on this issue. In 2015, *Agenda 2030* highlighted the need to protect the planet 'through sustainable consumption and production' and to 'foster peaceful, just and inclusive societies which are free from fear and violence' (Preamble). Changing unsustainable production and consumption patterns is vital and particularly important if other SDGs are to be achieved. SDG 12 responds to this sustainability challenge.

This chapter explores SDGs 11 and 12 together because they focus on the practical application of sustainability in a very human context. The chapter commences by explaining the international legal backdrop to these goals before examining the detail of the SDGs, targets and indicators and the role that they play in addressing the challenges confronting us.

6.2 The international law and policy context

A range of different areas of law are relevant to SDGs 11 and 12, including international environmental, planning and development laws, human rights law, trade and investment law, health, labour and migration law and corporate commercial laws. Yet without systemic change to the economic systems, social and environmental sustainability will be outweighed by commercial motivations and the laws that support them.[10]

Cities and settlements (SDG 11) are not the subject of any targeted international treaties but have received global institutional support through the UN

7 UNGA, *The Future We Want, Outcome Document of the UN Conference on Sustainable Development*, para 134.

8 UN, *Millennium Development Goals and Beyond 2015*, https://www.un.org/millenniumgoals/.

9 Kateřina Mitkidis and Adriana Šefčíková, 'SDG12: Ensure Sustainable Consumption and Productions Patterns' in Ilias Bantekas and Francesco Seatzu (eds), *The UN Sustainable Development Goals: A Commentary* (Oxford: OUP, 2024) 859.

10 Alessandra Arcuri and Enrico Partiti, 'SDG 12: Ensure Sustainable Consumption and Production Patterns' in J Ebbesson and E Hey (eds), *The Cambridge Handbook of The Sustainable Development Goals and International Law* (Cambridge: Cambridge University Press (2022) 305–306.

Human Settlements Programme (UN-Habitat) (established in 1975 and now a subsidiary organ of the General Assembly), which provides technical assistance with the aim of improving planning and governance as well as access to land, housing and basic services.[11] Cities and settlements have also been the focus of a series of UN Conferences on Human Settlements (commencing with Habitat I in 1976).[12] In 2016, at the UN Conference on Housing and Sustainable Urban Development (Habitat III), the *New Urban Agenda* was adopted and sets out a vision that embraces urbanisation to promote equity, human welfare and prosperity in the context of sustainable development.[13]

Although cities are often governed through local or provincial levels and in that sense are 'actors' which implement aspects of international law,[14] SDG 11 is mostly focused on cities and settlements as places where people live and work rather than governance levels. Of relevance in this respect is international human rights law. For example, the *Universal Declaration of Human Rights* (1948) stated that '[e]veryone has the right to a standard of living . . . including . . . housing' (Article 25). The *International Covenant on Economic, Social and Cultural Rights* (1966) (ICESCR) confirms the right of everyone to 'an adequate standard of living . . . including adequate . . . housing, and to the continuous improvement of living conditions' (Article 11), as well as 'safe and healthy working conditions' (Article 7(b)). Other human rights treaties relevant to the issue of safety in cities and settlements and access to transport include the *Convention on the Elimination of All Forms of Discrimination Against Women* (1979), *UN Convention on the Rights of the Child* (1989) and the *Convention on the Rights of Persons with Disabilities* (2006).

Environmental soft law instruments include some references to urban areas. For example, the *Stockholm Declaration* (1972) included a principle that '[p]lanning must be applied to human settlements and urbanization with a view to avoiding adverse effects on the environment and obtaining maximum social, economic and environmental benefits for all' (Principle 15). The only treaty explicitly mentioned in SDG 11 is the *World Heritage Convention* (1972), which provides a regime for the recognition, protection and presentation of natural and cultural sites of outstanding universal value.[15] Therefore, this treaty is relevant for only a small number of special places within cities and settlements. Nevertheless, UNESCO has established programmes and networks focused on cities, which were consolidated in 2019 into the UNESCO Cities Platform.[16]

11 UN Habitat, https://unhabitat.org/.
12 UN, *Conferences: Habitat*, https://www.un.org/en/conferences/habitat.
13 UN Habitat, *The New Urban Agenda*, https://habitat3.org/the-new-urban-agenda/.
14 Du Plessis (2022) 282.
15 UNESCO, *World Heritage Convention*, https://whc.unesco.org/en/convention/.
16 UNESCO, *Sustainable Cities*, https://www.unesco.org/en/sustainable-cities.

Several other treaties, whilst not referring explicitly to cities, do mention local and subnational levels, as well as the participation of local communities and populations in decision making: the *Paris Agreement* (2015) (Articles 7 and 11) and *UN Convention to Combat Desertification* (1994) (Articles 3, 5 and 10), for example. The final aspect of environmental law of relevance is the emerging area of disaster law. The Sendai Framework on Disaster Risk Reduction 2015–2030, also mentioned in the SDG, relates to natural hazards and those induced by human processes (such as climate change) and their prevention and reduction, as well as preparedness for them.[17]

As noted in Section 6.1, cities are places of economic activity, wealth and business, which implicates international trade, finance and investment laws. Yet the World Trade Organization (WTO) does not explicitly refer to SDGs 11 in its publications on the WTO and the SDGs.[18] The World Bank was involved with the housing agenda as early as 1972, when it formulated a policy on urbanisation and committed to directly assisting specific urban centres.[19] In the 1980s the World Bank increasingly focused on cities as actors,[20] including in its Urban, Disaster Risk Management, Resilience and Land Global Practice.[21]

Far greater explicit references can be found in international law in relation to consumption and production. The outcome document of the UN Conference on Environment and Development (Rio Conference), *The Future We Want* (1992), noted that 'changing unsustainable and promoting sustainable patterns of consumption and production . . . [are] essential requirements for sustainable development' (para 4). In addition, the *Rio Declaration* (1992) included the principle that 'States should reduce and eliminate unsustainable patterns of production and consumption' (Principle 8). Yet sustainable consumption and production can be linked to the earlier *Stockholm Declaration* (1972) (Principle 5 on the use of non-renewable resources and Principles 6–7 on prevention of harm).[22] SDG 12 does not refer to any particular treaties although one target refers to the UN 10-Year Framework of Programmes on Sustainable Consumption and Production Patterns (2014) (Target 12.1). This

17 UNDRR, *Sendai Framework on Disaster Risk Reduction 2015–2030*, https://www.undrr.org/publication/sendai-framework-disaster-risk-reduction-2015-2030.

18 See WTO, *The WTO and the Sustainable Development Goals*, https://www.wto.org/english/thewto_e/coher_e/sdgs_e/sdgs_e.htm.

19 Hannah Birkenkötter, 'SDG 12: Ensure Sustainable Consumption and Production Patterns' in Ilias Bantekas and Francesco Seatzu (eds), *The UN Sustainable Development Goals: A Commentary* (Oxford: OUP, 2024) 804.

20 Birkenkötter (2024).

21 World Bank Group, *Building Sustainable Cities & Communities*, https://www.worldbank.org/en/topic/sustainable-communities.

22 UNGA, *Report of the United Nations Conference on the Human Environment, Containing the Stockholm Declaration* (1972), https://documents.un.org/doc/undoc/gen/nl7/300/05/pdf/nl730005.pdf.

framework seeks to accelerate a change to more sustainable consumption and production by supporting national policies and activities; it includes programmes on a range of relevant topics, including sustainable public procurement, incorporation of sustainability into consumer education and sustainable construction and food systems.[23]

Specific treaties have focused on banning the production of certain dangerous substances and managing trade in others. For example, when science demonstrated that chlorofluorocarbons (CFCs) were causing a hole in the ozone layer, the global community adopted the *Vienna Convention for the Protection of the Ozone Layer* (1985) and the related *Montreal Protocol on Substances that Deplete the Ozone Layer* (1987).[24] The *Montreal Protocol* includes a phase-out plan for production and consumption of ozone-depleting substances, including CFCs. The *Basel Convention on the Control of Transboundary Movements of Hazardous Wastes and Their Disposal* (1989) includes obligations to report on measures to reduce or eliminate the production of hazardous waste but does not mandate their implementation (see Article 13(3)(h)).[25] The *Rotterdam Convention on the Prior Informed Consent Procedure for Certain Hazardous Chemicals and Pesticides in International Trade* (1998) lists certain chemicals and provides for transparency in their international trade to protect human and environmental health, with some substances being banned or severely restricted.[26] The *Stockholm Convention on Persistent Organic Pollutants* (2001) responded to scientific data indicating that persistent organic pollutants (POPs) are a significant threat to human and environmental health, prohibiting the production of some chemicals and requiring production reductions for others (Article 3).[27]

These three treaties focus on chemicals and hazardous waste, and yet the waste problem extends further. The global problem of plastic pollution has steadily attracted greater global attention, and in 2022 the international community agreed to commence negotiations for a new treaty.[28] Relevantly, the draft text includes measures addressing production, distribution and consumption, including reduction, reuse, recycling, repurposing and disposal.[29] If adopted, this will become the first global treaty comprehensively covering each stage of the plastic lifecycle. Other documents, such as the OECD's

23 For the full text of the Framework, see https://sdgs.un.org/publications/10-year-framework-programmes-sustainable-consumption-and-production-patterns-10yfp.
24 UNEP, *Ozone Treaties*, https://ozone.unep.org/.
25 See Basel Convention, https://www.basel.int/.
26 See Rotterdam Convention, https://www.pic.int/.
27 See Stockholm Convention, https://chm.pops.int/.
28 UNEP, *Intergovernmental Negotiating Committee (INC) on Plastic Pollution*, https://www.unep.org/inc-plastic-pollution.
29 The current draft text is available via the UNEP INC website and at https://wedocs.unep.org/bitstream/handle/20.500.11822/45858/Compilation_Text.pdf.

Guidelines on Multinational Enterprises (2023), encourage businesses to adoption sustainable consumption and production patterns. The *Guidelines* note that '[r]esource efficiency promotes more efficient and effective use of resources and materials . . . [and] . . . circular economy approaches are . . . one of the means available to achieve sustainable development' (para 73).[30]

International trade law is also relevant because the World Trade Organization rules require states not to discriminate between 'like' products, and those manufactured in more sustainable ways would be considered 'like' more conventionally made products. This may therefore create a barrier to sustainable production and consumption.[31] The WTO allows only limited exceptions where certain products or services are necessary to protect human, animal or plant life or if they relate to the conservation of exhaustible natural resources.[32] These limited exceptions are difficult to apply successfully in practice,[33] despite the aim of sustainable development being mentioned in the Preamble to the WTO Agreement (1994).[34] As earlier in this section, the WTO does not explicitly refer to SDG 12 on its website to link its work to the SDGs.[35]

Similarly, investment laws tend to favour economic goals over social and environmental ones.[36] Foreign direct investment can finance sustainable development, yet it can also support unsustainable consumption and production.[37] Foreign direct investment is arranged through bilateral agreements which vary considerably in their content with no imperative to ensure sustainability or environmentally friendly outcomes.

6.3 SDG 11 – sustainable cities and communities

SDG 11 is focused on inclusive, safe, resilient and sustainable cities and settlements. Notably, no reference is made to good governance – accountability, transparent, efficient and effective local government – nor to trade or human

30 OECD, *Guidelines for Multinational Enterprises on Responsible Business Conduct* (Paris: OECD Publishing, 2023).

31 WTO, *Principles of the Trading System,* https://www.wto.org/english/thewto_e/whatis_e/tif_e/fact2_e.htm.

32 *General Agreement on Tariffs and Trade* (1994), Articles 20(b) and (g). For the full text, see WTO Legal Texts, https://www.wto.org/english/docs_e/legal_e/legal_e.htm.

33 Mitkidis and Šefčíková (2024) 867.

34 WTO, *Marrakesh Agreement Establishing the World Trade Organization,* https://www.wto.org/english/docs_e/legal_e/04-wto_e.htm.

35 See WTO, *The WTO and the Sustainable Development Goals*, https://www.wto.org/english/thewto_e/coher_e/sdgs_e/sdgs_e.htm.

36 Stuart Bruce and Jorge E Viñuales, 'SDG 7' in J Ebbesson and E Hey (eds), *The Cambridge Handbook of The Sustainable Development Goals and International Law* (Cambridge: Cambridge University Press, 2022) 202.

37 See examples in Arcuri and Partiti (2022) 316.

rights law. Yet this is the only SDG that mentions heritage, despite its importance for socio-cultural sustainability.[38]

Goal 11. Make cities and human settlements inclusive, safe, resilient and sustainable

Targets	*Indicators*
11.1 By 2030, ensure access for all to adequate, safe and affordable housing and basic services and upgrade slums	*11.1.1 Proportion of urban population living in slums, informal settlements or inadequate housing*
11.2 By 2030, provide access to safe, affordable, accessible and sustainable transport systems for all, improving road safety, notably by expanding public transport, with special attention to the needs of those in vulnerable situations, women, children, persons with disabilities and older persons	*11.2.1 Proportion of population that has convenient access to public transport, by sex, age and persons with disabilities*
11.3 By 2030, enhance inclusive and sustainable urbanization and capacity for participatory, integrated and sustainable human settlement planning and management in all countries	*11.3.1 Ratio of land consumption rate to population growth rate* *11.3.2 Proportion of cities with a direct participation structure of civil society in urban planning and management that operate regularly and democratically*
11.4 Strengthen efforts to protect and safeguard the world's cultural and natural heritage	*11.4.1 Total per capita expenditure on the preservation, protection and conservation of all cultural and natural heritage, by source of funding (public, private), type of heritage (cultural, natural) and level of government (national, regional, and local/ municipal)*
11.5 By 2030, significantly reduce the number of deaths and the number of people affected and substantially decrease the direct economic losses relative to global gross domestic product caused by disasters, including water-related disasters, with a focus on protecting the poor and people in vulnerable situations	*11.5.1 Number of deaths, missing persons and directly affected persons attributed to disasters per 100,000 population* *11.5.2 Direct economic loss attributed to disasters in relation to global gross domestic product (GDP)* *11.5.3 (a) Damage to critical infrastructure and (b) number of disruptions to basic services, attributed to disasters*

(*Continued*)

38 Although traditional knowledge – related to cultural heritage – is included in Target 2.5.

(Continued)

Targets	*Indicators*
11.6 By 2030, reduce the adverse per capita environmental impact of cities, including by paying special attention to air quality and municipal and other waste management	*11.6.1 Number of deaths, missing persons and directly affected persons attributed to disasters per 100,000 population* *11.6.2 Direct economic loss attributed to disasters in relation to global gross domestic product (GDP)* *11.6.3 (a) Damage to critical infrastructure and (b) number of disruptions to basic services, attributed to disasters*
11.7 By 2030, provide universal access to safe, inclusive and accessible, green and public spaces, in particular for women and children, older persons and persons with disabilities	*11.7.1 Average share of the built-up area of cities that is open space for public use for all, by sex, age and persons with disabilities* *11.7.2 Proportion of persons victim of non-sexual or sexual harassment, by sex, age, disability status and place of occurrence, in the previous 12 months*
11.a Support positive economic, social and environmental links between urban, peri-urban and rural areas by strengthening national and regional development planning	*11.a.1 Number of countries that have national urban policies or regional development plans that (a) respond to population dynamics; (b) ensure balanced territorial development; and (c) increase local fiscal space*
11.b By 2020, substantially increase the number of cities and human settlements adopting and implementing integrated policies and plans towards inclusion, resource efficiency, mitigation and adaptation to climate change, resilience to disasters, and develop and implement, in line with the Sendai Framework for Disaster Risk Reduction 2015-2030, holistic disaster risk management at all levels	*11.b.1 Number of countries that adopt and implement national disaster risk reduction strategies in line with the Sendai Framework for Disaster Risk Reduction 2015–2030* *11.b.2 Proportion of local governments that adopt and implement local disaster risk reduction strategies in line with national disaster risk reduction strategies*
11.c Support least developed countries, including through financial and technical assistance, in building sustainable and resilient buildings utilizing local materials	*11.c.1 No suitable replacement indicator was proposed. The global statistical community is encouraged to work to develop an indicator that could be proposed for the 2025 comprehensive review. See E/CN.3/2020/2, paragraph 23*

6.3.1 Inclusive

Targets 11.1 and 11.2 seek to provide housing and transport, respectively, for *all* people. Although the wording changes slightly, both targets refer to 'safe' and 'affordable'. Interestingly, 11.2 adds accessibility and that special attention should be given to people in vulnerable positions as well as women, children, the elderly and those with disabilities. No such addition is included in Target 11.1 regarding housing. Target 11.7 is about inclusive green and public spaces, with inclusive here relating to accessibility. Target 11.3 is constructed differently but also refers to inclusiveness, here in terms of urbanisation with particular reference to participatory processes in planning and management.

6.3.2 Safe

Safe cities are the subject of Targets 11.1 and 11.2 in relation to housing and transport, as well as Target 11.7, which is specifically focused on accessible green and public spaces. Such places are needed to ensure socio-cultural sustainability, including for recreation, and are measured in Indicator 11.7.1 as a share of all city space. The safety aspect is measured in Indicator 11.7.2, which captures physical or sexual harassment in such places, which is particularly relevant to women and children but does not capture less harmful safety aspects.

6.3.3 Resilient

Resilience is often linked with disaster risk reduction, and Target 11.5 does so by seeking to significantly reduce the impacts of disasters on people. Disasters are not defined but presumably relate to natural events and/or those exacerbated by human conduct. Resilience is also at the core of Target 11.b, which encourages policies and plans that implement the *Sendai Framework* outlined in Section 6.2. Global financial and technical capacity building for resilient building is the focus of Target 11.c, with a valuable inclusion of 'utilizing local materials', which in turn can lead to more local economic growth.

6.3.4 Other sustainability measures

Target 11.4 is an outlier but broadly relates to social sustainability by seeking to better protect world heritage sites. This target could equally be seen as focused on inclusivity or resilience. Environmental sustainability is the focus of Target 11.6, which is aimed at reducing the impact of human settlements, including both solid waste and particulate matter. Target 11.a seeks to advance policies and plans that support sustainable development in urban, peri-urban and rural areas. It is one of the only targets to specifically mention rural settlements outside cities. Capacity building for sustainable cities is included in Target 11.c, as noted previously.

6.4 SDG 12 – responsible consumption and production

A specific SDG focused on consumption and production is critical for sustainable human futures. Nevertheless, the targets largely focus on production efficiency (with only a couple addressing consumption) are softly worded and weaken from target to indicator.[39] The following sections are divided into sustainable practices, waste and capacity building.

Goal 12. Ensure sustainable consumption and production patterns

Targets	*Indicators*
12.1 Implement the 10-year framework of programmes on sustainable consumption and production, all countries taking action, with developed countries taking the lead, taking into account the development and capabilities of developing countries	*12.1.1 Number of countries developing, adopting or implementing policy instruments aimed at supporting the shift to sustainable consumption and production*
12.2 By 2030, achieve the sustainable management and efficient use of natural resources	*12.2.1 Material footprint, material footprint per capita, and material footprint per GDP* *12.2.2 Domestic material consumption, domestic material consumption per capita, and domestic material consumption per GDP*
12.3 By 2030, halve per capita global food waste at the retail and consumer levels and reduce food losses along production and supply chains, including post-harvest losses	*12.3.1 (a) Food loss index and (b) food waste index*
12.4 By 2020, achieve the environmentally sound management of chemicals and all wastes throughout their life cycle, in accordance with agreed international frameworks, and significantly reduce their release to air, water and soil in order to minimize their adverse impacts on human health and the environment	*12.4.1 Number of parties to international multilateral environmental agreements on hazardous waste, and other chemicals that meet their commitments and obligations in transmitting information as required by each relevant agreement* *12.4.2 (a) Hazardous waste generated per capita; and (b) proportion of hazardous waste treated, by type of treatment*
12.5 By 2030, substantially reduce waste generation through prevention, reduction, recycling and reuse	*12.5.1 National recycling rate, tons of material recycled*

(*Continued*)

39 Des Gasper, Amod Shar and Sunil Tankha, 'The Framing of Sustainable Consumption and Production in SDG 12' (2019) 10(1) *Global Policy* 83.

(Continued)

Targets	*Indicators*
12.6 Encourage companies, especially large and transnational companies, to adopt sustainable practices and to integrate sustainability information into their reporting cycle	*12.6.1 Number of companies publishing sustainability reports*
12.7 Promote public procurement practices that are sustainable, in accordance with national policies and priorities	*12.7.1 Number of countries implementing sustainable public procurement policies and action plans*
12.8 By 2030, ensure that people everywhere have the relevant information and awareness for sustainable development and lifestyles in harmony with nature	*12.8.1 Extent to which (i) global citizenship education and (ii) education for sustainable development are mainstreamed in (a) national education policies; (b) curricula; (c) teacher education; and (d) student assessment*
12.a Support developing countries to strengthen their scientific and technological capacity to move towards more sustainable patterns of consumption and production	*12.a.1 Installed renewable energy-generating capacity in developing and developed countries (in watts per capita)*
12.b Develop and implement tools to monitor sustainable development impacts for sustainable tourism that creates jobs and promotes local culture and products	*12.b.1 Implementation of standard accounting tools to monitor the economic and environmental aspects of tourism sustainability*
12.c Rationalize inefficient fossil-fuel subsidies that encourage wasteful consumption by removing market distortions, in accordance with national circumstances, including by restructuring taxation and phasing out those harmful subsidies, where they exist, to reflect their environmental impacts, taking fully into account the specific needs and conditions of developing countries and minimizing the possible adverse impacts on their development in a manner that protects the poor and the affected communities	*12.c.1 Amount of fossil-fuel subsidies (production and consumption) per unit of GDP*

6.4.1 Sustainable practices

Target 12.1 specifically refers to the 10-Year Framework discussed in Section 6.2. In this sense the target squarely builds off a global initiative already in place and importantly requires developed countries to take the lead (along similar lines to Target 8.4). Target 12.2 is one of the very broad and vague aims with limited indicators assessing progress. Target 12.6 is one of the only goals that explicitly refers to companies. In this context it is about encouraging corporations to adopt sustainable practices and to report, with Indicator 12.6.1 focused on published sustainability reports. The government sector is the focus of Target 12.7, in particular sustainable procurement practices. These two targets should facilitate sustainable supply chains. Making information accessible to all people everywhere so that they can build sustainable lifestyles is captured in Target 12.8. The indicators relate to sustainable development in education, which will be important to shift consumption patterns.

6.4.2 Waste

Targets 12.3 and 12.4 focus specifically on reducing waste. Target 12.3 addresses food waste, which is critical to the achievement of SDG 2 as well as Target 11.6. The 'environmentally sound management' of chemicals and all wastes is the focus of Target 12.4, although the legal frameworks set out in Section 6.2 are not mentioned. Indicator 12.4.2 measures only hazardous waste, which may not account for plastics and other inert materials. Nevertheless, Target 12.5 seeks to substantially reduce all waste generation through prevention, reduction, recycling and reuse, all of which are critical to circular economy agenda and whole-lifecycle initiatives.

6.4.3 Capacity building

Target 12.a seeks to build scientific and technological capacity for sustainable consumption and production in developing countries. Clearly, this capacity is essential if consumption and production patterns are to change, yet the indicator only focuses on renewable energy. Target 12.b is narrow and relates to sustainable tourism and tools to monitor the impacts, presumably as this industry is seen as a potential option to attract non-consumptive economic benefits from nature without impacting it. Finally Target 12.c is about rationalising harmful subsidies, market distortions and taxation arrangements that encourage wasteful consumption. Surprisingly, no mention is made of the WTO or other trade and investment laws that could assist with this.

6.5 Progressing SDGs 11 and 12

SDGs 11 and 12 are both challenging goals. Neither was addressed in any meaningful way in the MDGs, and therefore these aims are relatively new. As set out in Section 6.2, both of these SDGs require input from different sectors and across multiple areas of law, policy and management. Cities and settlements are often led by poorly resourced local governments, which must contend with growing populations with increased social and environmental risks. Making the fundamental changes needed to achieve sustainable production and consumption will similarly involve multiple sectors and competing pressures.

6.5.1 Linkages between the SDGs

Cities and settlements are places where people aspire to live in safety and with adequate facilities, and in this respect SDG 11 intersects with SDG 1 (poverty), SDG 3 (health and well-being), SDG 4 (education), SDG 5 (gender equity), SDG 6 (water and sanitation), SDG 7 (energy), SDG 10 (inequality) and SDG 16 (peaceful and inclusive societies). In terms of places where people work, SDG 1 is relevant to SDG 8 (employment), SDG 9 (industry and innovation) and SDG 12 (consumption and production). Specific targets such as 11.6 (environmental impact of cities including waste management) link directly with the aims of SDGs 13, 14 and 15. In terms of cities and settlements as governance levels, SDG 11 links to other goals that promote participation of people and communities: SDGs 16 and 17 in particular, as well as SDGs 5 and 6.

The topic of waste links SDGs 11 and 12 through, for example, Targets 11.6 and 12.5. SDG 12 is squarely linked with environmental goals (SDGs 13, 14 and 15), as well as SDG 7 (water) and SDG 8 (in relation to renewable energy), as it seeks to reduce the environmental footprint of goods and services. The references to food waste in SDG 12 are also directly relevant to SDG 2 (ending hunger). There are some tensions and potential trade-offs as sustainable production and consumption are likely to increase the cost of goods and services and could exacerbate poverty (SDG 1) and inequalities (SDG 10).

6.5.2 The role of law and policy

The only specific law mentioned in SDGs 11 and 12 is in Target 11.4, relating to the World Heritage Convention, although Target 12.4 refers to 'agreed international frameworks' for chemicals and waste (which were outlined in Section 6.2). This is perhaps unsurprising given the limited international law in relation to cities, settlements, consumption and production. There are, however, many areas of law implicated by the targets. In relation to cities and settlements, planning law, waste management and pollution laws and human rights laws referred to in Section 6.2. Criminal law will be relevant to safety in terms of protection from other people and disaster law regarding other hazards. Investment law is also relevant to support least developed countries. Sustainable consumption and production will require commercial incentives which could be implemented through law, as well as pollution laws, production standards and financial and regulatory support for the circular economy agenda.

6.6 Conclusion

SDGs 11 and 12 relate to the application of sustainable development in cities, in settlements and in production and consumption. The UN High Level Political Forum on Sustainable Development (HLPF), in 2023, referred explicitly to the implementation of the *New Urban Agenda* to make cities and settlements inclusive, safe, resilient and sustainable.[40] The HLPF also recommitted to 'fundamental changes in our consumption and production patterns', recognising that 'zero-waste initiatives can contribute' (para 38(i)). Yet in 2024, only 25 per cent of SDG 11 was on track, with another 25 per cent stagnating or regressing.[41] Furthermore, 40 per cent of SDG 12 was on track, but 60 per cent is stagnating or regressing. The HLPF referred to promoting a 'systemic shift', but something more will be required to achieve these SDGs by 2030.[42]

40 UNGA, *Political Declaration of the High-Level Political Forum on Sustainable Development Convened Under the Auspices of the General Assembly* (2023), https://www.un.org/en/conferences/SDGSummit2023/political-declaration, para 38(h).

41 UNGA, *Progress Towards the Sustainable Development Goals* (2024), https://unstats.un.org/sdgs/files/report/2024/SG-SDG-Progress-Report-2024-advanced-unedited-version.pdf. See also Our World in Data, *SDG Tracker: Measuring Progress Towards the Sustainable Development Goals* (2023), https://ourworldindata.org/sdgs.

42 UNGA, *Political Declaration* (2023), para 9.

13
CLIMATE
ACTION

14
LIFE
BELOW WATER

15
LIFE
ON LAND

Timeline – international environmental law, climate change law and law of the sea

Non Binding Initiatives	*Date*	*Legally Binding Conventions*
	1946	International Convention on the Regulation of Whaling
International Maritime Organization (IMO) is established	**1948**	
IUCN Red List is created	**1964**	
	1971	Convention on Wetlands of International Importance (Ramsar Convention)
UN Conference on the Human Environment (Stockholm Conference) UN Environment Programme (UNEP) is established	**1972**	Convention on the Prevention of Marine Pollution by Dumping of Wastes (London Convention) World Heritage Convention
	1973	Convention on International Trade in Endangered Species (CITES) International Convention for the Prevention of Pollution from Ships (MARPOL 73/78)
	1979	Convention on Migratory Species (CMS)
	1982	UN Convention on the Law of the Sea (UNCLOS)
UN creates the World Commission on Environment and Development	**1983**	
Our Common Future ('Brundtland Report') is published	**1987**	Montreal Protocol on Ozone Depleting Substances
Intergovernmental Panel on Climate Change (IPCC) is created	**1988**	
UN Conference on Environment & Development (Rio Conference)	**1992**	UN Framework Convention on Climate Change (UNFCCC) UN Convention on Biological Diversity (CBD) UN Convention to Combat Desertification (UNCCD)
	1997	Kyoto Protocol
	1998	Rotterdam Convention on the Prior Informed Consent Procedure for Certain Hazardous Chemicals and Pesticides in International Trade
Adoption of Millenium Development Goals (MDGs)	**2000**	

(*Continued*)

(Continued)

Non Binding Initiatives	*Date*	*Legally Binding Conventions*
	2001	Stockholm Convention on Persistent Organic Pollutants
UN Decade on Biodiversity 2011-2020	**2011**	
	2013	Minamata Convention on Mercury
Adoption of the Sustainable Development Goals (SDGs)	**2015**	Paris Agreement
UN Decade on Ecosystem Restoration	**2021**	
CBD parties adopt Kunming-Montreal Global Biodiversity Framework (GBF)	**2022**	Negotiations commence for a new plastic pollution treaty
Global Framework on Chemicals	**2023**	Implementing Agreement under UNCLOS on the Conservation and Sustainable Use of Biological Diversity of Areas Beyond National Jurisdictions (BBNJ Agreement/ High Seas Treaty)

7 Environment protection, conservation and climate change

SDGs 13, 14 and 15

7.1 Background

The world is currently facing triple planetary crises of human-induced climate change, pollution and biodiversity loss,[1] the extent of which has led to the coining of the term 'Anthropocene'.[2] Environmental issues emerged as global concerns in the 1970s when the environmental movement swept around the world.[3] Since then, there have been myriad United Nations (UN) conferences on environmental issues, hundreds of international treaties and multilateral environmental agreements and countless environmental initiatives from the global to the local scale. Yet environmental indicators continue to worsen, with the climate and extinction crises rapidly approaching planetary boundaries.[4] Thankfully, the permanent loss of oceanic species is not as high as on land, with only 15 marine extinctions to date.[5] Yet the outlook is poor, with the collapse of some fish stocks due to overharvesting, and a decreasing proportion of remaining stocks are fished within sustainable levels.[6] Marine plastic debris is a growing concern, with predictions that by 2050 there will be more plastic than fish in our oceans.[7]

1 UN Climate Change, 'What Is the Triple Planetary Crisis?' *UNFCCC Blog*, April 13, 2022, https://unfccc.int/news/what-is-the-triple-planetary-crisis.
2 For an explanation of the term Anthropocene, see National Geographic, 'Anthropocene', https://education.nationalgeographic.org/resource/anthropocene/.
3 Lorraine Elliott, 'History of the Environmental Movement' *Brittanica*, October 11, 2024, https://www.britannica.com/topic/environmentalism/History-of-the-environmental-movement.
4 Stockholm Resilience Centre, Planetary boundaries, https://www.stockholmresilience.org/research/planetary-boundaries.html.
5 D McCauley et al., 'Marine Defaunation: Animal Loss in the Global Ocean' (2015) 347(6219) *Science* 1255641. Yet even here the authors show that the trajectory is not positive.
6 FAO, *FAO Report: Global Fisheries and Aquaculture Production Reaches a New Record High* (June 7, 2024), https://www.fao.org/newsroom/detail/fao-report-global-fisheries-and-aquaculture-production-reaches-a-new-record-high/en.
7 UNESCO, *Ocean Plastic Pollution an Overview: Data and Statistics,* https://oceanliteracy.unesco.org/plastic-pollution-ocean/.

DOI: 10.4324/9781003583981-7

In *Agenda 2030*, the UN highlighted 'Planet' as a key focus and its determination to protect it 'from degradation, including through sustainable consumption and production, sustainably managing its natural resources and taking urgent action on climate change, so that it can support the needs of the present and future generations'.[8] Although MDG 7 had included two short targets focused on sustainable development and biodiversity loss, the SDGs expanded the ambition to three separate goals (covering climate change, life on land and in the ocean) together with 27 targets.

This chapter explores SDGs 13, 14 and 15 together, as they are all focused on environmental matters. The chapter commences by explaining the international legal backdrop to these goals before examining the detail of the SDGs, targets and indicators and the role that law can play in addressing environmental challenges confronting us.

7.2 The international law and policy context

SDGs 13, 14 and 15 are underpinned by the exponential growth in international environmental law since the 1970s. Early treaties focused on managing species as resources (such as the *International Convention on the Regulation of Whaling* (1946)), but conservation focused regimes included the *Convention on International Trade in Endangered Species* (1973) and *Convention on Migratory Species* (1979),[9] and later the *Convention on Biological Diversity* (CBD) (1992). Pollution concerns led to the *Convention on the Prevention of Marine Pollution by Dumping of Wastes* (1972) and *International Convention for the Prevention of Pollution from Ships* (MARPOL 73/78). The *UN Convention on the Law of the Sea* (UNCLOS) (1982) codified many rules and obligations relating to our ocean and the expansion of global fishery regulation.[10] Habitat loss resulted in the adoption of the *World Heritage Convention* (1972) and the *Ramsar Convention on Wetlands* (1973) in response. Climate change issues emerged in the 1980s, leading to the negotiation of the *UN Framework Convention on Climate Change* (UNFCCC) (1992).

Of these instruments only a select few included quantified targets. Under the umbrella of the UNFCCC, and its broad ambition to hold greenhouse gas emissions to 1990 levels (Art 4(2)(b)), the *Kyoto Protocol* set out binding emission reduction targets for 39 nations (the 24 original OECD members, the European Union and 14 countries with economies in transition) for the

8 *Agenda 2030*, para 2.
9 UNEP, *Species+*, https://www.speciesplus.net/.
10 For further detail about UNCLOS, see UN, *Division for Ocean Affairs and the Law of the Sea*, https://www.un.org/depts/los/convention_agreements/convention_overview_convention.htm.

period 2008–2012.[11] With most countries not meeting their emission reduction targets, and polarised debate around requiring all nations to mitigate their emissions, shortly after *Agenda 2030* was adopted, the *Paris Agreement* was endorsed by the global community. It became the next implementing agreement under the UNFCCC, yet it does not include any quantitative targets.[12] The CBD established the Aichi Biodiversity Targets, including five strategic goals and 20 targets to be achieved by 2020.[13] Again these were not met, and the CBD concluded the subsequent *Kunming-Montreal Global Biodiversity Framework* (GBF) in 2022 as the successor to the *Aichi Biodiversity Targets*, and it does include goals and targets to be achieved by 2050.[14]

Therefore, unlike some other areas of law related to the SDGs, in this case the global community had already endorsed targets in the context of international treaties. SDGs 13, 14 and 15 build upon these global efforts and international law obligations by providing quantitative and qualitative goals, some of which are clearly aligned with the international environmental law convention goals and targets. However, only the UNFCCC is specifically named.

7.3 SDG 13 – climate action

Climate change is one of the greatest challenges of sustainable development and was rightly given its own SDG.[15] However, the climate change and development agendas had developed separately, and the SDGs were negotiated at the same time as the *Paris Agreement* process.[16] Therefore, detailed measures to address climate change were included in the latter, and SDG 13 includes only five indicators, the least of any of the goals.[17] The five targets and indicators address both capacity building and other implementation measures.

11 UN Climate Change, *What Is the Kyoto Protocol?* https://unfccc.int/kyoto_protocol. The Doha Amendment to the Kyoto Protocol extended the commitment period to 2020, in which 37 countries had binding targets.

12 UN Climate Change, *What Is the Paris Agreement?* https://unfccc.int/process-and-meetings/the-paris-agreement.

13 CBD, *Aichi Biodiversity Targets*, https://www.cbd.int/sp/targets.

14 CBD, *The Biodiversity Plan*, https://www.cbd.int/gbf.

15 No such goal had been included in the MDGs despite international laws being in place since 1992.

16 Daniel Bodansky, 'SDG13: Take Urgent Action to Combat Climate Change and Its Impacts' in J Ebbesson and E Hey (eds), *The Cambridge Handbook of The Sustainable Development Goals and International Law* (Cambridge: Cambridge University Press, 2022) 327.

17 SDG 13 includes a footnote acknowledging that the UNFCCC is the primary forum for negotiating global responses to climate change: *Agenda 2030*, para 23.

Goal 13. Take urgent action to combat climate change and its impacts*
* Acknowledging that the United Nations Framework Convention on Climate Change is the primary international, intergovernmental forum for negotiating the global response to climate change.

Targets	*Indicators*
13.1 Strengthen resilience and adaptive capacity to climate-related hazards and natural disasters in all countries	*13.1.1 Number of deaths, missing persons and directly affected persons attributed to disasters per 100,000 population* *13.1.2 Number of countries that adopt and implement national disaster risk reduction strategies in line with the Sendai Framework for Disaster Risk Reduction 2015–2030* *13.1.3 Proportion of local governments that adopt and implement local disaster risk reduction strategies in line with national disaster risk reduction strategies*
13.2 Integrate climate change measures into national policies, strategies and planning	*13.2.1 Number of countries with nationally determined contributions, long-term strategies, national adaptation plans and adaptation communications, as reported to the secretariat of the United Nations Framework Convention on Climate Change* *13.2.2 Total greenhouse gas emissions per year*
13.3 Improve education, awareness-raising and human and institutional capacity on climate change mitigation, adaptation, impact reduction and early warning	*13.3.1 Extent to which (i) global citizenship education and (ii) education for sustainable development are mainstreamed in (a) national education policies; (b) curricula; (c) teacher education; and (d) student assessment*
13.a Implement the commitment undertaken by developed-country parties to the United Nations Framework Convention on Climate Change to a goal of mobilizing jointly $100 billion annually by 2020 from all sources to address the needs of developing countries in the context of meaningful mitigation actions and transparency on implementation and fully operationalize the Green Climate Fund through its capitalization as soon as possible	*13.a.1 Amounts provided and mobilized in United States dollars per year in relation to the continued existing collective mobilization goal of the $100 billion commitment through to 2025*

(*Continued*)

(Continued)

Targets	*Indicators*
13.b Promote mechanisms for raising capacity for effective climate change-related planning and management in least developed countries and small island developing States, including focusing on women, youth and local and marginalized communities	*13.b.1 Number of least developed countries and small island developing States with nationally determined contributions, long-term strategies, national adaptation plans and adaptation communications, as reported to the secretariat of the United Nations Framework Convention on Climate Change*

7.3.1 Capacity building

Target 13.1 is an example of the softer, non-quantitative wording seen throughout SDG 13. The aim is to 'strengthen' resilience and capacity to adapt to climate change, added to which is Target 13.3, focused on 'improving' capacity, education and awareness raising. These verbs are open to significant interpretation, and yet the indicators highlight the narrow criteria that are used to measure progress.

Target 13.2 addresses governance initiatives, calling for climate change to be integrated across policies, strategies and planning instruments at the national level. The aim is to avoid action on climate change separate from the drivers and impacts of it. The two indicators measure global action: total number of nations with relevant policies/plans and combined emissions.

7.3.2 Implementation measures

Specific reference is made in Target 13.a to the Green Climate Fund, agreed to by the parties to the UNFCCC in the 2009 *Copenhagen Accord*. This fund is now operational and supports developing countries to 'accelerate transformative climate action'.[18] Target 13.b is similar but focuses on strengthening planning and management in small island developing states (SIDS) as well as least developed nations. The former are at greater risk from sea level rise, and the least developed nations have the most limited resources to respond to climate change. In both cases these states tend not to have contributed significantly to climate change, as they are not significant greenhouse gas emitters, yet they will face the greatest impacts. Here the indicator measures the number of countries with relevant plans/policies, similar to the first indicator for Target 13.2.

18 Green Climate Fund, https://www.greenclimate.fund/.

7.4 SDG 14 – life below water

Multiple international treaties include commitments focused on oceans however, few include data collection, monitoring and reporting obligations, and none contain legally binding targets. As highlighted in section 7.2, only the CBD has specific, measurable, time-limited goals, and SDG 14 incorporates some of these. A review of the ten SDG 14 targets demonstrates that they cover four key areas – pollution, conservation, climate change and fisheries – as well as implementation measures.

Goal 14. Conserve and sustainably use the oceans, seas and marine resources for sustainable development

Targets	*Indicators*
14.1 By 2025, prevent and significantly reduce marine pollution of all kinds, in particular from land-based activities, including marine debris and nutrient pollution	*14.1.1 (a) Index of coastal eutrophication; and (b) plastic debris density*
14.2 By 2020, sustainably manage and protect marine and coastal ecosystems to avoid significant adverse impacts, including by strengthening their resilience, and take action for their restoration in order to achieve healthy and productive oceans	*14.2.1 Number of countries using ecosystem-based approaches to managing marine areas*
14.3 Minimize and address the impacts of ocean acidification, including through enhanced scientific cooperation at all levels	*14.3.1 Average marine acidity (pH) measured at agreed suite of representative sampling stations*
14.4 By 2020, effectively regulate harvesting and end overfishing, illegal, unreported and unregulated fishing and destructive fishing practices and implement science-based management plans, in order to restore fish stocks in the shortest time feasible, at least to levels that can produce maximum sustainable yield as determined by their biological characteristics	*14.4.1 Proportion of fish stocks within biologically sustainable levels*
14.5 By 2020, conserve at least 10 per cent of coastal and marine areas, consistent with national and international law and based on the best available scientific information	*14.5.1 Coverage of protected areas in relation to marine areas*

(*Continued*)

(Continued)

Targets	*Indicators*
14.6 By 2020, prohibit certain forms of fisheries subsidies which contribute to overcapacity and overfishing, eliminate subsidies that contribute to illegal, unreported and unregulated fishing and refrain from introducing new such subsidies, recognizing that appropriate and effective special and differential treatment for developing and least developed countries should be an integral part of the World Trade Organization fisheries subsidies negotiation	*14.6.1 Degree of implementation of international instruments aiming to combat illegal, unreported and unregulated fishing*
14.7 By 2030, increase the economic benefits to Small Island developing States and least developed countries from the sustainable use of marine resources, including through sustainable management of fisheries, aquaculture and tourism	*14.7.1 Sustainable fisheries as a proportion of GDP in small island developing States, least developed countries and all countries*
14.a Increase scientific knowledge, develop research capacity and transfer marine technology, taking into account the Intergovernmental Oceanographic Commission Criteria and Guidelines on the Transfer of Marine Technology, in order to improve ocean health and to enhance the contribution of marine biodiversity to the development of developing countries, in particular small island developing States and least developed countries	*14.a.1 Proportion of total research budget allocated to research in the field of marine technology*
14.b Provide access for small-scale artisanal fishers to marine resources and markets	*14.b.1 Degree of application of a legal/regulatory/policy/institutional framework which recognizes and protects access rights for small-scale fisheries*
14.c Enhance the conservation and sustainable use of oceans and their resources by implementing international law as reflected in UNCLOS, which provides the legal framework for the conservation and sustainable use of oceans and their resources, as recalled in paragraph 158 of The Future We Want	*14.c.1 Number of countries making progress in ratifying, accepting and implementing through legal, policy and institutional frameworks, ocean-related instruments that implement international law, as reflected in the United Nations Convention on the Law of the Sea, for the conservation and sustainable use of the oceans and their resources*

7.4.1 Pollution

Target 14.1 focuses on preventing and reducing marine pollution, especially from land-based sources. Significant global efforts have been made to prevent, reduce and control marine pollution from all sources since the 1970s, with international treaties obliging states to 'protect and preserve the marine environment', outlawing the deliberate 'dumping of waste' at sea and mandating gear and equipment to prevent oil spills.[19] UNCLOS includes obligations for states to address land-based marine pollution, but no specific global rules have been adopted.[20] Yet plastic debris and nutrient pollution are significant challenges.[21] The addition of 'including marine debris and nutrient pollution' as the only indicator responds to the plastics issues as well as water quality impacts from agricultural runoff (such as fertilisers).

7.4.2 Conservation of marine ecosystems and areas

Target 14.2 is time limited and was to be achieved by 2020. Undoubtedly, most nations have undoubtedly taken some steps to sustainably manage and restore damaged, coastal and marine ecosystems, but not all laws refer explicitly to 'ecosystem-based approaches' as required by Indicator 14.2.1.[22] Target 14.5 was also to be achieved by 2020 and requires at least 10 per cent of marine and coastal areas to be conserved in accordance with science and law. This target aligns with the CBD Aichi target (now superseded by the GBF) and is clearly measurable with global databases such as the MPA Atlas tracking results.[23]

7.4.3 Climate change

Climate change is at the heart of Target 14.3, yet there is ambiguity in the indicator, as the places where ocean acidification was to be measured were yet to be agreed upon. This target is related to the mitigation of emissions, which are a focus of SDG 13.

19 Relevant instruments include the *UN Convention on the Law of the Sea*, *London Convention* and Protocol and the MARPOL Convention. Erika Techera and Joy McCann, *The Unruly Ocean: Law and Justice in the World's Oceans Seas and Shorelines* (Abingdon: Routledge, 2025), particularly chapter 9, 'Waste: Discharge, Dumping and Debris at Sea'.

20 Negotiations are underway for a new treaty on plastic pollution, much of which comes from land: UNEP, *Intergovernmental Negotiating Committee on Plastic Pollution*, https://www.unep.org/inc-plastic-pollution.

21 Advocates for International Development, *SDG 14: Life Below Water – A Legal Guide* (London: A4ID, 2023), https://sdglegalinitiative.a4id.org/sdg-legal-guide/.

22 UNGA, *Global Indicator Framework for the Sustainable Development Goals and Targets of the 2030 Agenda for Sustainable Development* (2017).

23 Marine Conservation Institution, *Marine Protection Atlas*, https://mpatlas.org/.

7.4.4 Fishery regulation

SDG 14.4 requires effective fishery regulation to be in place by 2020. Although most nations have fishery laws, and there are multiple international fishery instruments, illegal, unreported and unregulated fishing is a major concern. The indicator for this target is the global proportion of fish stocks within biologically sustainable levels, yet the FAO has found this percentage is decreasing. Target 14.6 is one of the strongly worded targets, requiring prohibition of fishery subsidies which support over-capacity, over-fishing and illegal fishing and undermine sustainability. In 2022, the WTO adopted an agreement banning harmful fishery subsidies – a major step forward for SDG 14.[24] The indicator, however, only focuses on illegal fishing. Target 14.7 could also undermine sustainability but increase economic benefits to SIDS and least developed countries derived from marine resources. Reference is made to fisheries as well as aquaculture and tourism (important, as it does not require the extraction of fish from the ocean), yet the indicator only relates to fishing.

7.4.5 Implementation measures

Target 14.a supports funding for the production and sharing of marine scientific knowledge and transfer of technology to support efforts to improve ocean health, particularly in the most vulnerable nations. Here a specific intergovernmental organisation and guideline document is named.[25] Target 14.b seeks to improve market access for artisanal fishers – those involved in small-scale fishing, including for subsistence, who provide local food and livelihoods. Interestingly the indicator measures the implementation of legal and regulatory frameworks essential to support these fishers. Target 14.c makes specific reference to the ratification and implementation of UNCLOS. The majority of nations are a party to this convention, with implementation being varied given the number and flexibility of obligations.

7.5 SDG 15 – life on land

Despite international law developments, human population growth and industrialisation continue to impact living and non-living resources. SDG 15 includes targets and indicators for specific groups such as forests and mountains, for land health and habitats more broadly and species and ecosystems,

24 WTO, *Agreement on Fisheries Subsidies*, https://www.wto.org/english/tratop_e/rulesneg_e/fish_e/fish_e.htm.

25 UNESCO, *Marine Policy*, https://www.ioc.unesco.org/en/marine-policy.

as well as implementation measures, focused on conservation and sustainable use.

Goal 15. Protect, restore and promote sustainable use of terrestrial ecosystems, sustainably manage forests, combat desertification, and halt and reverse land degradation and halt biodiversity loss

Target	*Indicator*
15.1 By 2020, ensure the conservation, restoration and sustainable use of terrestrial and inland freshwater ecosystems and their services, in particular forests, wetlands, mountains and drylands, in line with obligations under international agreements	*15.1.1 Forest area as a proportion of total land area* *15.1.2 Proportion of important sites for terrestrial and freshwater biodiversity that are covered by protected areas, by ecosystem type*
15.2 By 2020, promote the implementation of sustainable management of all types of forests, halt deforestation, restore degraded forests and substantially increase afforestation and reforestation globally	*15.2.1 Progress towards sustainable forest management*
15.3 By 2030, combat desertification, restore degraded land and soil, including land affected by desertification, drought and floods, and strive to achieve a land degradation-neutral world	*15.3.1 Proportion of land that is degraded over total land area*
15.4 By 2030, ensure the conservation of mountain ecosystems, including their biodiversity, in order to enhance their capacity to provide benefits that are essential for sustainable development	*15.4.1 Coverage by protected areas of important sites for mountain biodiversity 15.4.2 (a) Mountain Green Cover Index and (b) proportion of degraded mountain land*
15.5 Take urgent and significant action to reduce the degradation of natural habitats, halt the loss of biodiversity and, by 2020, protect and prevent the extinction of threatened species	*15.5.1 Red List Index*
15.6 Promote fair and equitable sharing of the benefits arising from the utilization of genetic resources and promote appropriate access to such resources, as internationally agreed	*15.6.1 Number of countries that have adopted legislative, administrative and policy frameworks to ensure fair and equitable sharing of benefits*
15.7 Take urgent action to end poaching and trafficking of protected species of flora and fauna and address both demand and supply of illegal wildlife products	*15.7.1 Proportion of traded wildlife that was poached or illicitly trafficked*

(*Continued*)

(Continued)

Target	*Indicator*
15.8 By 2020, introduce measures to prevent the introduction and significantly reduce the impact of invasive alien species on land and water ecosystems and control or eradicate the priority species	*15.8.1 Proportion of countries adopting relevant national legislation and adequately resourcing the prevention or control of invasive alien species*
15.9 By 2020, integrate ecosystem and biodiversity values into national and local planning, development processes, poverty reduction strategies and accounts	*15.9.1 (a) Number of countries that have established national targets in accordance with or similar to Aichi Biodiversity Target 2 of the Strategic Plan for Biodiversity 2011–2020 in their national biodiversity strategy and action plans and the progress reported towards these targets; and (b) integration of biodiversity into national accounting and reporting systems, defined as implementation of the System of Environmental-Economic Accounting*
15.a Mobilize and significantly increase financial resources from all sources to conserve and sustainably use biodiversity and ecosystems	*15.a.1 (a) Official development assistance on conservation and sustainable use of biodiversity; and (b) revenue generated and finance mobilized from biodiversity-relevant economic instruments*
15.b Mobilize significant resources from all sources and at all levels to finance sustainable forest management and provide adequate incentives to developing countries to advance such management, including for conservation and reforestation	*15.b.1 (a) Official development assistance on conservation and sustainable use of biodiversity; and (b) revenue generated and finance mobilized from biodiversity-relevant economic instruments*
15.c Enhance global support for efforts to combat poaching and trafficking of protected species, including by increasing the capacity of local communities to pursue sustainable livelihood opportunities	*15.c.1 Proportion of traded wildlife that was poached or illicitly trafficked*

7.5.1 Conservation

Conservation is at the heart of the majority of SDG 15. Target 15.1 centres on ensuring conservation of various land types, yet the indicators only relate to measurable areas of forests and freshwater. Mountains are the specific focus of Target 15.4, and here the indicator refers to a particular index as a data point.[26] Target 15.3 focuses on halting degradation of land more broadly through desertification (loss of land fertility), floods and drought. Reducing degradation of habitats, and ending the extinction of biodiversity, is the aim of Target 15.5. Again, a well-known index is used to measure progress on species loss.[27] Species loss is further supported by Target 15.7, calling for an end to poaching and illegal trade in wildlife.[28] Similarly, Target 15.8 addresses a major impact and driver of native species loss. Although there is no global treaty on invasive species, there are some relevant agreements on introduction via shipping and transport, for example.[29] The final target on conservation is about integration of ecosystem and biodiversity values in planning, and the indicator refers specifically to the Aichi targets and environmental accounting.

7.5.2 Sustainable use

There is no binding international agreement on forests, and so Target 15.2 is important in encouraging sustainable use of forests and requiring states to cease the most damaging activities. Unlike other indicators in SDG 15, Target 15.2.1 is relatively vague and difficult to measure. Target 15.6 builds on the CBD obligations relating to access and benefit sharing of genetic resources.[30] The indicator relates to law and policy measures states have adopted, many of which may be related to the CBD.

7.5.3 Implementation

The three targets support mobilising funding and resources for conservation and sustainable use. Targets 15.a and 15.b relate to funding, with the letter being focused specifically on forests. Target 15.c is aimed at activating global support to halt poaching and trafficking and thus supports Target 15.7 – with the indicator being identical.

7.6 Progressing SDGs 13, 14 and 15

Environmental quality is one of the pillars of sustainable development and the 'planet' ambitions set out in the Preamble to *Agenda 2030*. Notably, there

26 Our World in Data, *Mountain Green Cover Index*, https://ourworldindata.org/grapher/mountain-green-cover-index.
27 IUCN, *Red List*, https://www.iucnredlist.org/.
28 Although not mentioned in the indicator, there are global bodies that monitor trafficking: UNEP, *WCMC*, https://www.unep-wcmc.org/en and TRAFFIC, https://www.traffic.org/.
29 IMO, *Ballast Water Management*, https://www.imo.org/en/OurWork/Environment/Pages/BallastWaterManagement.aspx.
30 CBD, *The Nagoya Protocol on Access and Benefit-Sharing*, https://www.cbd.int/abs/default.shtml.

are only three environmental SDGs. The strong emphasis on SIDS and least developed nations, as well as local communities and small-scale and artisanal workers, implements another fundamental aim of the *Agenda 2030* – that no one is left behind.

7.6.1 Linkages across the SDGs[31]

Climate change, sustainable oceans and life on land are all inherently linked. As noted in section 7.3, SDG 13 intentionally did not add measurable targets, given the simultaneous negotiation process for the *Paris Agreement*. Yet SDG 13 includes the concepts of mitigation and adaptation and focuses strongly on capacity building as well as the need for funding. Both SDGs 14 and 15 refer to 'life', and yet several of the targets address broader environmental concerns. Many of the targets focus on well-known issues of pollution and fishery management, and, relevantly, in relation to the latter, there is an effort to address subsidies, which can undermine conservation efforts. Yet some other targets are in tension, such as support for small-scale fishers whose livelihoods could be impacted if marine-protected areas are set aside for conservation.[32] Balancing the consumptive use of biodiversity with its conservation is an inherent challenge, and the SDGs have a far greater task in doing so in the context of human rights and broader societal pressures and goals.[33]

Of the other goals, SDGs 1, 2 and 11 all refer explicitly to climate change. Possibly, all of the other SDGs can contribute to mitigating the impacts of climate change: in particular, SDGs 6, 9, 11 and 12 relating to sustainable energy, infrastructure, cities and consumption and production. In turn, SDG 7 (energy), SDG 8 (economic growth), SDG 9 (resilient infrastructure) and SDG 12 (consumption and production) must be undertaken in climate responsible ways. Climate change can also exacerbate and undermine poverty (SDG 1), food insecurity (SDG 2), human health (SDG 3) and inequality (SDGs 5 and 10). Simultaneously, climate change has the potential to impact the achievement of all other SDGs, such as SDG 6 in relation to clean water and sanitation, SDG 11 on cities and settlements and SDG 16 on justice. Similarly, SDGs 14 and 15 are inherently linked to human well-being both in terms of

31 For a broader examination of linkages with SDG 14, see International Council for Science, *A Guide to SDG Interactions: From Science to Implementation* (2017), https://council.science/wp-content/uploads/2017/05/SDGs-Guide-to-Interactions.pdf.

32 For further discussion of tensions and conflicts, see Karen Scott, 'SDG 14: Conserve and Sustainably Use the Oceans, Seas and Marine Resources for Sustainable Development' in J Ebbesson and E Hey (eds), *The Cambridge Handbook of the Sustainable Development Goals and International Law* (Cambridge: Cambridge University Press, 2022) 354–375.

33 For further discussion, see Elisa Morgera, 'SDG15: Protect, Restore and Promote Sustainable Use of Terrestrial Ecosystems, Sustainably Manage Forests, Combat Desertification, and Halt and Reverse Land Degradation and Halt Biodiversity Loss' in J Ebbesson and E Hey (eds), *The Cambridge Handbook of the Sustainable Development Goals and International Law* (Cambridge: Cambridge University Press, 2022) 376–398.

food production and sustainable agriculture (SDG 2), clean water and sanitation (SDG 6) and human health (SDG 3). The conservation targets within SDG 15 are directly linked with Target 2.5 and genetic diversity for agriculture, as well as SDG 6 focused on water. More broadly, SDG 14 and 15 support healthy environments that are critical for human health and well-being (SDG 3) and resilience (SDG 11) and underpin sustainable consumption and production (SDG 12), as well as the aims of SDGs 16 and 17.

7.6.2 The role of law and policy

SDG 13 makes specific reference to the UNFCCC and SDG 14 to UNCLOS. Law is overtly referred to in Targets 14.5 and 14.c. Law, policy and institutions also feature in Indicators 14.b.1 and 14.c.1. Target 13.2 focuses on the integration of climate change in national policies and strategies, and Indicators 15.6.1 and 15.8.1 measure achievements with reference to the adoption of legislation.

Clearly, environmental law has the most significant role to play in advancing many of the targets most relevantly, preventing pollution and invasive species, managing ecosystems and land, sustainable forestry and fishing, conserving areas, prohibiting poaching and fishing subsidies and implementing international law (all targets in SDGs 14 and 15).

7.7 Conclusion

SDGs 13, 14 and 15 all focus on environmental health, and by addressing environmental concerns, they are crucial if we are to respond effectively to the twin climate and extinction crises. It is concerning that none of the targets in SDG 13 are on track to be achieved, and only a small proportion of those included in SDGs 14 and 15 are.[34] As demonstrated in other chapters in this book, these three SDGs can support the achievement of other goals, but their achievement is challenged by competing pressures. The UN High Level Political Forum on Sustainable Development (HLPF) reaffirmed that 'climate change is one of the greatest challenges of our time'[35] and that 'the impacts of climate change [becoming] more pronounced'.[36] If SDG 13 in particular, as well as SDGs 14 and 15, are to get back on track, urgent and profound action is needed.

34 UNGA, *Progress Towards the Sustainable Development Goals* (2024), https://unstats.un.org/sdgs/files/report/2024/SG-SDG-Progress-Report-2024-advanced-unedited-version.pdf. See also Our World in Data, *SDG Tracker: Measuring Progress Towards the Sustainable Development Goals* (2023), https://ourworldindata.org/sdgs.

35 UNGA, *Political Declaration of the High-Level Political Forum on Sustainable Development Convened Under the Auspices of the General Assembly* (2023), https://www.un.org/en/conferences/SDGSummit2023/political-declaration, para 7.

36 UNGA, *Political Declaration of the High-Level Political Forum on Sustainable Development Convened Under the Auspices of the General Assembly* (2023), para 8.

Timeline – developments relating to peace, justice and partnerships

Non-Binding Actions	*Date*	*Binding International Law*
International Court of Justice established	**1945**	UN Charter
Universal Declaration of Human Rights	**1948**	
	1965	International Convention on the Elimination of All Forms of Racial Discrimination
	1966	International Covenant on Economic, Social and Cultural Rights
		International Covenant on Civil and Political Rights

(*Continued*)

(Continued)

Non-Binding Actions	*Date*	*Binding International Law*
	1979	Convention on the Elimination of all Forms of Discrimination against Women
	1984	Convention against Torture and Other Cruel, Inhuman or Degrading Treatment or Punishment
Declaration on the Right to Development	**1986**	
	1989	UN Convention on the Rights of the Child
	1990	Convention on the Protection of the Rights of All Migrant Workers and Members of their Families
	1993	Chemical Weapons Convention
United Nations Office on Drugs and Crime established	**1997**	
Rome Statute establishing the International Criminal Court	**1998**	Aarhus Convention on Access to Information, Public Participation in Decision-Making and Access to Justice in Environmental Matters
UN Declaration and Programme of Action on a Culture of Peace	**1999**	
	2000	UN Convention against Transnational Organized Crime
	2001	Protocol against the Illicit Manufacturing of and Trafficking in Firearms, their Parts and Components and Ammunition
	2003	UN Convention against Corruption Protocol to Prevent, Suppress and Punish Trafficking in Persons, especially Women and Children
	2004	Protocol against the Smuggling of Migrants by Land, Sea and Air
Doha Declaration on Financing for Development	**2008**	
Declaration on the Rule of Law at National and International Levels	**2012**	
	2014	Arms Trade Treaty
Regional Agreement on Access to Information, Public Participation and Justice in Environmental Matters in Latin America and the Caribbean (Escazú Agreement)	**2018**	
	2019	2030 Agenda Partnership Accelerator

8 Peace, justice and partnerships

SDGs 16 and 17

8.1 Background

Peace, security and international cooperation are key objectives of the United Nations (UN) articulated in its Charter (1945). Although data suggests that the number of deaths from war is falling, violent conflict continues to rise.[1] Peace and justice are critical to the achievement of many SDGs, with violence, for example, linked to poverty.[2] Furthermore, lack of legal identity (a focus of SDG 16) is also related to poverty as well as marginalisation, and addressing the issue is fundamental to the achievement of human rights.[3] These and related areas have defied efforts to solve them, and some have worsened.[4]

Agenda 2030 acknowledged the importance of 'peaceful, just and inclusive societies' (para 3) and 'a world of universal respect for human rights and human dignity, the rule of law, justice, quality and non-discrimination' (para 8) and 'one in which democracy, good governance and the rule of law . . . are essential' (para 9). SDGs 16 and 17 respond to these commitments and build on global infrastructure to address known problems. SDG 16 focuses on legal issues and the political organisation of societies and includes targets that connect with pre-existing international law obligations.

1 UN SDGs, *Goal 16: Promote Just, Peaceful and Inclusive Societies,* https://www.un.org/sustainabledevelopment/peace-justice/.

2 Homicide rates are far higher where income inequality is high: Advocates for International Development, *SDG 16: Peace, Justice and Strong Institutions – A Legal Guide* (London: A4ID, 2021) 7.

3 UNDP, *Having a Legal Identity is Fundamental to Human Rights*, https://www.undp.org/africa/blog/having-legal-identity-fundamental-human-rights.

4 Official development assistance has helped to support developing nations, but these countries already face rising external debt levels which have worsened following the COVID-19 pandemic: UN SDGs, *Goal 17: Revitalize the Global Partnership for Sustainable Development*, https://www.un.org/sustainabledevelopment/globalpartnerships/.

DOI: 10.4324/9781003583981-8

SDG 17 is inherently associated with all the other goals, as it focuses on implementation of the SDGs through partnerships needed for sustainable development.

Because their achievement is essential for all other goals, SDGs 16 and 17 are explored in the same chapter. They address fundamental conditions (rights and institutions) as well as implementation and cooperation for sustainable development. The chapter commences by explaining the international legal backdrop to these goals before examining the details of the SDGs, targets and indicators and the role of law in facilitating their success.

8.2 The international law and policy context

Perhaps more than any other goal, SDG 16 is underpinned by international law instruments and obligations. The *UN Charter* (1945), *Universal Declaration on Human Rights* (1948), *International Covenant on Economic, Social and Cultural Rights* (ICESCR) (1966), *International Covenant on Civil and Political Rights* (ICCPR) (1966), and *UN Convention on the Rights of the Child* (CRC) (1989), for example, all focus on ending violence, with the right to life being central. Reducing violence also links directly to criminal law as well humanitarian law (laws of war). In addition, the UDHR and CRC both reinforce the right to a legal identity, and the UDHR and the *Declaration on the Right to Development* (1986) support sustainable development.

The rule of law is linked to many of the international law instruments referred to previously and more broadly to access to justice, non-discrimination, fairness and human rights. The *Declaration on the Rule of Law at National and International Levels* (2012) notes that 'the rule of law and development are strongly interrelated and mutually reinforcing, [and] that the advancement of the rule of law . . . is essential for . . . sustainable development' (para 7). It has also been noted that 'good governance is key to sustainable development'.[5] Both of these concepts are mentioned in SDG 16. Other relevant international law includes the access to justice instruments which support the exercise of legal rights including through courts (Aarhus Convention and Escazú Agreement) and focused treaties such as the *UN Convention against Corruption* (2003).

Much of SDG 17 relates to trade, finance and technology. Relevant international institutions include the World Trade Organization as well as other

5 Pål Wrange, 'SDG 16: Promote Peaceful and Inclusive Societies for Sustainable Development, Provide Access to Justice for All and Build Effective, Accountable and Inclusive Institutions at All Levels' in J Ebbesson and E Hey (eds), *The Cambridge Handbook of The Sustainable Development Goals and International Law* (Cambridge: Cambridge University Press, 2022) 413.

relevant international laws include trade and investment rules. In addition, the *Doha Declaration on Financing for Development* (2008) is relevant, as it supports the mobilisation of global and domestic financial resources, international financial and technical cooperation for development, external debt and the need to address systemic issues in international monetary, financial and trading systems.

Capacity building has featured in international law for several decades and is clearly supported by broader UN goals and instruments to address equality amongst nations and to assist developing and least developed nations. It adds to the existing body of laws that support peace, justice and strong institutions.

8.3 SDG 16 – peace, justice and strong institutions

SDG 16 is easily divided into its three core components of peaceful and inclusive societies, justice and strong institutions, although there is overlap between them.

Goal 16. Promote peaceful and inclusive societies for sustainable development, provide access to justice for all and build effective, accountable and inclusive institutions at all levels

Targets	*Indicators*
16.1 Significantly reduce all forms of violence and related death rates everywhere	*16.1.1 Number of victims of intentional homicide per 100,000 population, by sex and age* *16.1.2 Conflict-related deaths per 100,000 population, by sex, age and cause* *16.1.3 Proportion of population subjected to (a) physical violence, (b) psychological violence and/or (c) sexual violence in the previous 12 months* *16.1.4 Proportion of population that feel safe walking alone around the area they live after dark*
16.2 End abuse, exploitation, trafficking and all forms of violence against and torture of children	*16.2.1 Proportion of children aged 1–17 years who experienced any physical punishment and/or psychological aggression by caregivers in the past month* *16.2.2 Number of victims of human trafficking per 100,000 population, by sex, age and form of exploitation* *16.2.3 Proportion of young women and men aged 18–29 years who experienced sexual violence by age 18*

(*Continued*)

(Continued)

Targets	*Indicators*
16.3 Promote the rule of law at the national and international levels and ensure equal access to justice for all	*16.3.1 Proportion of victims of (a) physical, (b) psychological and/or (c) sexual violence in the previous 12 months who reported their victimization to competent authorities or other officially recognized conflict resolution mechanisms* *16.3.2 Unsentenced detainees as a proportion of overall prison population* *16.3.3 Proportion of the population who have experienced a dispute in the past two years and who accessed a formal or informal dispute resolution mechanism, by type of mechanism*
16.4 By 2030, significantly reduce illicit financial and arms flows, strengthen the recovery and return of stolen assets and combat all forms of organized crime	*16.4.1 Total value of inward and outward illicit financial flows (in current United States dollars)* *16.4.2 Proportion of seized, found or surrendered arms whose illicit origin or context has been traced or established by a competent authority in line with international instruments*
16.5 Substantially reduce corruption and bribery in all their forms	*16.5.1 Proportion of persons who had at least one contact with a public official and who paid a bribe to a public official, or were asked for a bribe by those public officials, during the previous 12 months* *16.5.2 Proportion of businesses that had at least one contact with a public official and that paid a bribe to a public official, or were asked for a bribe by those public officials during the previous 12 months*
16.6 Develop effective, accountable and transparent institutions at all levels	*16.6.1 Primary government expenditures as a proportion of original approved budget, by sector (or by budget codes or similar) 16.6.2 Proportion of population satisfied with their last experience of public services*
16.7 Ensure responsive, inclusive, participatory and representative decision-making at all levels	*16.7.1 Proportions of positions in national and local institutions, including (a) the legislatures; (b) the public service; and (c) the judiciary, compared to national distributions, by sex, age, persons with disabilities and population groups* *16.7.2 Proportion of population who believe decision making is inclusive and responsive, by sex, age, disability and population group*
16.8 Broaden and strengthen the participation of developing countries in the institutions of global governance	*16.8.1 Proportion of members and voting rights of developing countries in international organizations*

(*Continued*)

(Continued)

Targets	*Indicators*
16.9 By 2030, provide legal identity for all, including birth registration	*16.9.1 Proportion of children under 5 years of age whose births have been registered with a civil authority, by age*
16.10 Ensure public access to information and protect fundamental freedoms, in accordance with national legislation and international agreements	*16.10.1 Number of verified cases of killing, kidnapping, enforced disappearance, arbitrary detention and torture of journalists, associated media personnel, trade unionists and human rights advocates in the previous 12 months* *16.10.2 Number of countries that adopt and implement constitutional, statutory and/or policy guarantees for public access to information*
16.a Strengthen relevant national institutions, including through international cooperation, for building capacity at all levels, in particular in developing countries, to prevent violence and combat terrorism and crime	*16.a.1 Existence of independent national human rights institutions in compliance with the Paris Principles*
16.b Promote and enforce non-discriminatory laws and policies for sustainable development	*16.b.1 Proportion of population reporting having personally felt discriminated against or harassed in the previous 12 months on the basis of a ground of discrimination prohibited under international human rights law*

8.3.1 Peaceful and inclusive societies

SDG 16 refers explicitly to peaceful and inclusive societies rather than peace itself,[6] and Targets 16.1 and 16.2 both focus on peacefulness in the sense of reducing or ending violence.[7] It has been said, however, that peaceful 'means more than just the absence of conflict'.[8] Nevertheless, the scope of the targets captures a wide range of criminal activity. In addition, Target 16.4 addresses the challenge of flows of illicit monies and arms, as well as organised crime more broadly, which can sustain violence, terrorism and crime as well as undermining socio-economic development. Target 16.a supports the achievement of the other targets by encouraging states to strengthen institutions to prevent violence, terrorism and crime. Target 16.b provides the only direct reference to sustainable development in this goal.

6 Commented upon by Wrange (2022) in his chapter.

7 The first indicator for SDG 16.3 also assesses the number of people exposed to violence.

8 Advocates for International Development, *SDG 16* (2021).

8.3.2 Justice

Justice is engaged with in two senses: access to justice (i.e., courts and dispute resolution bodies) and, more broadly, fairness to all. Target 16.3 explicitly mentions justice for all in the context of the rule of law. The indicators for this target only focus on criminal justice: victims reporting violence, which relies upon them having trust in the authorities, and pre-sentencing detention of accused persons, which relates to effectiveness of the justice system. Target 16.10 relates, in part, to access to justice in relation to information, fundamental freedoms and law. Indicator 16.10.1 narrows the focus to freedom of the press and speech more broadly and 16.10.2 to justice more directly. Target 16.b is linked to law (and justice) through the reference to non-discrimination and the explicit mention of international human rights in the indicator (which is identical to Indicator 10.3.1). Wider conceptions of justice and fairness can be seen in Target 16.5 on reducing bribery and corruption, Target 16.9 relating to legal identity documents and 16.b on non-discrimination. Corruption has been noted as one of the largest impediments to achieving the SDGs.[9]

8.3.3 Institutions

Clearly, institutions are relevant to the achievement of all the SDGs, as it is through them that laws, policies and actions are developed and implemented. Institutions are explicitly referred to in Targets 16.6, 16.8 and 16.a; they are also implicit in Target 16.7. Target 16.8 recognises the inequality between states and that the participation of developing countries is critical for global governance. Target 16.6 refers to good governance principles of effectiveness, accountability and transparency, yet the indicators focus on effectiveness, although they do measure budget reliability and perceptions of accountability. Transparency is not defined but could be advanced through Target 16.10, as it encourages public access to information. However, Indicator 16.10.2 centres on the implementation of laws and policies and, as with other similar measures, it does not ensure quality. Target 16.7 includes most of the other principles of good governance by requiring decision-making be inclusive, participatory and representative, measured by quantitative indicators. Good governance also requires that everyone be treated equally before the law and that bribery and corruption (the focus of Target 16.5) be eradicated.

9 Advocates for International Development, *SDG 16* (2021) 12.

8.4 SDG 17 – partnerships for the goals

SDG 17 is related to implementation and therefore supports and underpins all other goals. The targets are divided under headings of finance, technology, capacity-building, trade and systemic issues, and these categories are used in the next sections.

Goal 17. Strengthen the means of implementation and revitalize the Global Partnership for Sustainable Development

Targets	*Indicators*
17.1 Strengthen domestic resource mobilization, including through international support to developing countries, to improve domestic capacity for tax and other revenue collection	*17.1.1 Total government revenue as a proportion of GDP, by source* *17.1.2 Proportion of domestic budget funded by domestic taxes*
17.2 Developed countries to implement fully their official development assistance commitments, including the commitment by many developed countries to achieve the target of 0.7 per cent of gross national income for official development assistance (ODA/GNI) to developing countries and 0.15 to 0.20 per cent of ODA/GNI to least developed countries; ODA providers are encouraged to consider setting a target to provide at least 0.20 per cent of ODA/GNI to least developed countries	*17.2.1 Net official development assistance, total and to least developed countries, as a proportion of the Organization for Economic Cooperation and Development (OECD) Development Assistance Committee donors' gross national income (GNI)*
17.3 Mobilize additional financial resources for developing countries from multiple sources	*17.3.1 Additional financial resources mobilized for developing countries from multiple sources 17.3.2 Volume of remittances (in United States dollars) as a proportion of total GDP*
17.4 Assist developing countries in attaining long-term debt sustainability through coordinated policies aimed at fostering debt financing, debt relief and debt restructuring, as appropriate, and address the external debt of highly indebted poor countries to reduce debt distress	*17.4.1 Debt service as a proportion of exports of goods and services*
17.5 Adopt and implement investment promotion regimes for least developed countries	*17.5.1 Number of countries that adopt and implement investment promotion regimes for developing countries, including the least developed countries*

(*Continued*)

(Continued)

Targets	*Indicators*
17.6 Enhance North-South, South-South and triangular regional and international cooperation on and access to science, technology and innovation and enhance knowledge sharing on mutually agreed terms, including through improved coordination among existing mechanisms, in particular at the United Nations level, and through a global technology facilitation mechanism	*17.6.1 Fixed broadband subscriptions per 100 inhabitants, by speed*
17.7 Promote the development, transfer, dissemination and diffusion of environmentally sound technologies to developing countries on favourable terms, including on concessional and preferential terms, as mutually agreed	17.7.1 Total amount of funding for developing countries to promote the development, transfer, dissemination and diffusion of environmentally sound technologies
17.8 Fully operationalize the technology bank and science, technology and innovation capacity-building mechanism for least developed countries by 2017 and enhance the use of enabling technology, in particular information and communications technology	17.8.1 Proportion of individuals using the Internet
17.9 Enhance international support for implementing effective and targeted capacity-building in developing countries to support national plans to implement all the Sustainable Development Goals, including through North-South, South-South and triangular cooperation	*17.9.1 Dollar value of financial and technical assistance (including through North-South, South-South and triangular cooperation) committed to developing countries*
17.10 Promote a universal, rules-based, open, non-discriminatory and equitable multilateral trading system under the World Trade Organization, including through the conclusion of negotiations under its Doha Development Agenda	*17.10.1 Worldwide weighted tariff-average*
17.11 Significantly increase the exports of developing countries, in particular with a view to doubling the least developed countries' share of global exports by 2020	*17.11.1 Developing countries' and least developed countries' share of global exports*

(*Continued*)

(Continued)

Targets	*Indicators*
17.12 Realize timely implementation of duty-free and quota-free market access on a lasting basis for all least developed countries, consistent with World Trade Organization decisions, including by ensuring that preferential rules of origin applicable to imports from least developed countries are transparent and simple, and contribute to facilitating market access	*17.12.1 Weighted average tariffs faced by developing countries, least developed countries and small island developing States*
17.13 Enhance global macroeconomic stability, including through policy coordination and policy coherence	*17.13.1 Macroeconomic Dashboard*
17.14 Enhance policy coherence for sustainable development	*17.14.1 Number of countries with mechanisms in place to enhance policy coherence of sustainable development*
17.15 Respect each country's policy space and leadership to establish and implement policies for poverty eradication and sustainable development	*17.15.1 Extent of use of country-owned results frameworks and planning tools by providers of development cooperation*
17.16 Enhance the Global Partnership for Sustainable Development, complemented by multi-stakeholder partnerships that mobilize and share knowledge, expertise, technology and financial resources, to support the achievement of the Sustainable Development Goals in all countries, in particular developing countries	*17.16.1 Number of countries reporting progress in multistakeholder development effectiveness monitoring frameworks that support the achievement of the Sustainable Development Goals*
17.17 Encourage and promote effective public, public-private and civil society partnerships, building on the experience and resourcing strategies of partnerships	*17.17.1 Amount in United States dollars committed to public-private partnerships for infrastructure*
17.18 By 2020, enhance capacity-building support to developing countries, including for least developed countries and small island developing States, to increase significantly the availability of high-quality, timely and reliable data disaggregated by income, gender, age, race, ethnicity, migratory status, disability, geographic location and other characteristics relevant in national contexts	*17.18.1 Statistical capacity indicators* *17.18.2 Number of countries that have national statistical legislation that complies with the Fundamental Principles of Official Statistics* *17.18.3 Number of countries with a national statistical plan that is fully funded and under implementation, by source of funding*

(*Continued*)

(Continued)

Targets	*Indicators*
17.19 By 2030, build on existing initiatives to develop measurements of progress on sustainable development that complement gross domestic product, and support statistical capacity-building in developing countries	*17.19.1 Dollar value of all resources made available to strengthen statistical capacity in developing countries* *17.19.2 Proportion of countries that (a) have conducted at least one population and housing census in the last 10 years; and (b) have achieved 100 per cent birth registration and 80 per cent death registration*

8.4.1 Finance

The five targets here include a strong thread of supporting developing countries: Targets 17.2, 17.3, 17.4 and 17.5 make overt reference to these nations. Notably, Targets 17.2 and (presumably) 17.5 put the onus on developed countries. Target 17.1 focuses on domestic financial resources and includes Indicator 17.1.2 relating to domestic taxation. These funds can be used to advance other national social, environmental and developmental goals and therefore are critical to the attainment of many goals. Corporate tax planning strategies that shift profits to lower tax locations negatively impact domestic government budgets. Target 7.2 includes the 0.7 per cent target which was first introduced in 1970 but has yet to be achieved,[10] and Target 7.3 seeks to mobilise further funding which will be needed to overcome inequalities between nations.

8.4.2 Technology

Targets 17.6 and 17.8 relate to technology, capacity building and sharing of knowledge, with indicators supporting internet access and use. Target 17.7 is broader as it is about promoting environmentally sound technology transfer to developing countries, and the indicator is related to funding for this aim.

8.4.3 Capacity building

Implementation of the SDGs is at the centre of Target 17.9, which seeks to enhance support for capacity-building through partnerships. The indicator is again a financial measure and inherently connected with Target 17.3.

10 Advocates for International Development, *SDG 17: Partnerships for the Goals – A Legal Guide* (London: A4ID, 2023) 5.

8.4.4 Trade

Again, these targets are focused on developing countries, including increasing their exports (17.11) and market access (17.12). Target 17.10 names the World Trade Organization under which an inclusive trading system should operate. However, global negotiations to reform the international trading system (commencing in 2001), including lowering trade barriers and revising trade rules, have not been concluded.[11]

8.4.5 Systemic issues

This section includes seven targets divided into policy and institutional coherence, multi-stakeholder partnerships and data, monitoring and accountability. Targets 17.14 and 17.5 relate to national policies generally (with one indicator highlighting the sovereignty of nations to develop their own policies) and 17.13 to economic policy more narrowly (with an indicator that is relatively opaque). The two partnership targets (17.6 and 17.7) focus on global efforts to achieve sustainable development as well as public–private partnerships, presumably between actors within and across various nations. Increasing access to accurate data is the aim of Target 17.18, added to which is Target 17.19 on data related to progress on sustainable development. Lack of reliable data hampers the assessment of the SDGs and may mask regression and/or progression.

8.5 Progressing SDGs 16 and 17

Peace, justice and partnerships are all foundational elements for sustainable development, and this is reflected in the linkages between SDGs 16 and 17 and other goals. Understanding the mutual benefits can help progress these SDGs. In addition, law has a critical role to play. Both SDGs 16 and 17 build upon a strong foundation of international law and in turn can benefit from law and policy tools. These two aspects are considered in further detail below.

8.5.1 Mutual support across the SDGs

Within SDG 16, there is a clear link between Target 16.9 (legal identity) and the protection of women and children from trafficking and other crimes (such as Targets 16.1 and 16.2). SDG 16 focuses heavily on inclusiveness, which is also relevant to many other SDGs and targets, including those focused specifically on developing nations and those which seek to ensure

11 WTO, *The Doha Round*, https://www.wto.org/english/tratop_e/dda_e/dda_e.htm.

equality. For example, Target 16.8 on participation of developing countries in global governance is well aligned with 10.6 about reducing inequality within and among countries (and, indeed, Indicator 16.8.1 is identical to 10.6.1). More specifically, organised crime (Target 16.4) undermines social and economic development, and therefore its suppression will benefit many other SDGs. Target 16.2 links with SDG 5.2 on violence, trafficking and sexual exploitation of women and girls, as well as Targets 8.7 (forced labour and modern slavery), 4.7 and 4.a (education). The provision of legal identity (Target 16.9) will assist in protecting children and women (SDGs 5 and 8) as well as other SDGs.

Several targets in SDG 17 are also mutually supportive, but some could possibly undermine each other. Target 17.3, for example, includes an indicator relating to increasing official development assistance, which could contribute to increased debt and thus undermine Target 17.4. Target 17.6 is about technology transfer and knowledge sharing, which also features in 14.a, and the provision of internet broadband (Indicators 17.6.1 and 17.8.1) will facilitate other information sharing.

8.5.2 The role of law and policy

The rule of law is explicitly referred to in Target 16.3 and non-discrimination laws in 16.b. The role of national legislation is specifically noted in Target 16.10 and Indicator 17.18.2. International law is highlighted in Target 16.10 and Indicator 16.b.1. Policies are directly mentioned in Targets 17.4, 17.13, 17.14 and 17.15.

Clearly, a well-functioning criminal justice system is necessary to reduce violence, human trafficking, abuse and exploitation (Targets 16.1, 16.2, 16.3, 16.10 and 16.a) and to prevent illicit activity (Target 16.4). Criminal and human rights law, institutions (including courts), access to information and legal services are vital for many of the targets in SDG 16. Human rights law is also relevant for institutions as an avenue to report and address abuses, including discrimination (Targets 16.a and 16.b). Law is needed to provide a framework for good governance (including in decision-making (Target 16.7)), which would create an enabling environment for public–private partnerships (Target 17.17), and to hold the public sector accountable in order to reduce corruption and bribery (Target 16.5). Legislation is also needed to establish legal identity documentation systems (Target 16.9). Similarly, law and policy can play a part in setting standards for institutions to ensure they are participatory, transparent and accountable (Target 16.6). Taxation and corporate law could be used to advance Target 17.1 by restricting companies from moving monies offshore, and finance laws could help to promote investment (Target 17.5). International trade law is essential for Target 17.10 and relevant for Targets 17.11 and 17.12.

8.5 Conclusion

SDGs 16 and 17 support the achievement of sustainable development and in many respects all of the other SDGs. As demonstrated in other chapters in this book, the targets and indicators narrow the scope of the two SDGs. Nevertheless, there are meaningful elements to measure progress towards the broader aims. Advancement on SDG 16 is disappointing, yet the story for SDG 17 is more positive, with a third of the targets on track to be achieved and a further third with moderate progress.[12] Yet the UN High Level Political Forum on Sustainable Development (HLPF) has acknowledged that the 'achievement of the SDGs is in peril'.[13] If all 17 SDGs are to be advanced, then greater attention must surely be given to these two SDGs given their central role in implementing sustainable futures.

12 UNGA, *Progress Towards the Sustainable Development Goals* (2024). See also Our World in Data, *SDG Tracker: Measuring Progress Towards the Sustainable Development Goals* (2023), https://ourworldindata.org/sdgs.

13 UNGA, *Political Declaration of the High-Level Political Forum on Sustainable Development Convened Under the Auspices of the General Assembly* (2023), para 8.

9 Achieving the SDGs

9.1 Introduction

The Sustainable Development Goals (SDGs) seek to 'stimulate action . . . in areas of critical importance for humanity and the planet', recognising that the 'interlinkages and integrated nature . . . are of crucial importance'.[1] Therefore, each and every SDG must be achieved for *Agenda 2030* to be effective. Yet more than halfway through the 15-year period to achieve the goals, the 2024 SDGs Report notes that 'the world is severely off track'.[2] This raises the question of what the United Nations (UN) has done to achieve the goals to date and what more the international community can do before 2030.

As none of the targets have yet been achieved, and none are entirely on track for 2030, increasing the ambition of the SDGs is not appropriate, and instead options must be identified to advance the SDGs as already set. Accelerating progress requires implementation of commitments already made, and this in turn may also involve greater cooperative activities. These aspects are explored in the following sub-sections below through a legal lens that aligns with earlier chapters of this book.

This chapter commences by examining progress to date, including the efforts made by the UN to raise awareness of the SDGs and assessments and reports on progress to date. The sections that follow outline planned actions as well as options to enhance cooperation and implementation. The chapter, and the book, ends with some concluding comments.

1 UNGA, *Transforming Our World: The 2030 Agenda for Sustainable Development* (2015), (*Agenda 2030*), Preamble.

2 UN, *Sustainable Development Goal Report 2024*, 4, https://dashboards.sdgindex.org.

DOI: 10.4324/9781003583981-9

9.2 Actions and progress

9.2.1 Communicating the SDGs

An examination of the SDG website demonstrates the UN efforts to raise awareness of the SDGs and communicate information about them and how to achieve them.[3] As well as setting out the targets, indicators and progress on each SDG, the website showcases 39 focal topic areas. The website also collates and makes accessible relevant publications, disseminates information on each member state including statements made by key national actors, and encourages engagement through events and webinars. In addition, the SDG Actions Platform provides a global registry of stakeholder actions, demonstrating action from the global to the local levels, including from governments, corporations, communities and individuals.[4]

Relevant to law and policy-making, the SDG website includes a section on inter-governmental processes. Just as UN conferences focused on sustainable development were hosted prior to the adoption of the SDGs, they have continued. Critically, the work of the High-Level Political Forum on Sustainable Development (HLPF) is included – explored in more detail in the following. Two other specific initiatives are highlighted: (1) the Multi-Stakeholder Forum on Science, Technology and Innovation (STI) for the SDGs and (2) the SAMOA Pathway relating to Small Island Developing States (SIDS).[5] There is also a section of the website devoted to building knowledge, capacity and resources around stakeholder engagement, as involving all groups at all levels is critical for both collaboration and implementation of activities that support the SDGs.

9.2.2 Assessing progress

For the SDGs to retain their aspirational value, it is important that progress be assessed and reported upon based on trusted data and methodologies. The HLPF was established in 2012, ahead of the adoption of the SDGs, as a platform for follow-up and review of the goals.[6] Key responsibilities including reviewing global progress, promoting accountability, fostering cooperation, providing guiding policy and supporting implementation.[7] HLPF meets annually, bringing together government representatives as well as other experts and stakeholders to review selected SDGs in detail. In addition, countries can

3 UN SDGs, https://sdgs.un.org/. See also each individual SDG and the 'Progress and Info' tabs.

4 The UN SDG Actions Platform is a publicly accessible, global registry of actions: https://sdgs.un.org/partnerships.

5 There is a whole section of the website devoted to SIDS.

6 UN, *High-Level Political Forum on Sustainable Development*, https://hlpf.un.org/.

7 UN HLPF, *Mandate and Functions*, https://hlpf.un.org/mandate-and-functions.

nominate for Voluntary National Reviews at these meetings. Every four years the HLPF is convened under the auspices of the UN General Assembly as the SDG Summit.[8] The HLPF website provides details of these meetings and summits, outcome documents and, importantly, the scope of upcoming meetings. For example, in 2025 the focus will be on 'Advancing sustainable, inclusive, science- and evidence-based solutions for the 2030 Agenda and its SDGs for leaving no one behind'. SDGs 3, 5, 8, 14 and 17 will be reviewed in depth. The HLPF meeting in 2026 will focus on 'Transformative, equitable, innovative and coordinated actions for the 2030 Agenda and its SDGs for a sustainable future for all', with SDGs 6, 7, 9, 11, and 17 to be reviewed in detail. The next SDG Summit will be held in 2027, in addition to the HLPF annual meeting, which will focus on 'Scaling up just transitions to achieving sustainable development, poverty eradication and the full implementation of the 2030 Agenda and its SDGs', with SDGs 4, 10, 12, 15 and 17 to be reviewed in depth.

As explained in section 9.2, the HLPF assesses global progress on the SDGs. Data for these assessments is based upon information gathered in relation to the SDG indicators. The indicators did not form part of *Agenda 2030* but rather were adopted later, in 2017.[9] Although comprehensive, it is clear from Chapters 2–8 that the ambition of the goals tends to be weakened in the targets and narrowed further in the indicators. It has been said that 'there is a tendency for indicators to become targets . . . since "what gets measured gets done" '.[10] Therefore, finding ways to sharpen the focus of indicators, and to adopt more where the target demands it, are ways in which they can be improved in the future. As noted in Chapter 1, the indicators are reviewed annually, and whilst work remains to be done, there is no doubt that improvements have been made with each review, such as filling gaps where indicators initially did not exist.[11]

Coupled with the indicators themselves is the necessity for accurate data, which is frequently lacking, problematic for many developing countries and particularly difficult for all nations in relation to illegal or illicit activity.[12] Mostly, official data is used to assess progress on the indicators, with sources including international organisations as well as household surveys and civil

8 SDG Summits have been held in 2019 and 2023 and are planned for 2025, 2026 and 2027.

9 UN General Assembly, *Work of the Statistical Commission Pertaining to the 2030 Agenda for Sustainable Development* (2017), Annex, https://documents.un.org/doc/undoc/gen/n17/207/63/pdf/n1720763.pdf.

10 Pål Wrange, 'SDG 16: Promote Peaceful and Inclusive Societies for Sustainable Development, Provide Access to Justice for All and Build Effective, Accountable and Inclusive Institutions at All Levels' in J Ebbesson and E Hey (eds), *The Cambridge Handbook of The Sustainable Development Goals and International Law* (Cambridge: CUP, 2022) 406.

11 UNGA, *Work of the Statistical Commission . . .*

12 It was noted that one third of the indicators lack data for the last three years: *The Sustainable Development Report 2024*, 4.

society organisations.[13] Improving data to support the global indicator framework was the focus of the *Cape Town Global Action Plan for Sustainable Development Data* (2017), which includes six strategic areas: (1) coordination and strategic leadership on data, (2) innovation and modernisation of national statistical systems, (3) strengthening basic statistical activities and programmes, (4) dissemination and use of sustainable development data, (5) multi-stakeholder partnerships and (6) resource mobilisation and statistical capacity building.[14] To these ends, the UN provides a number of resources relevant to measuring and assessing progress on the SDGs: the *SDG Global Database*,[15] the *UN Statistical Commission Metadata Repository*[16] and the *UN Data Commons for the SDGs*.[17] In addition, improved UN resources include the new *UN Data Platform*, which brings together data from across the United Nations.[18] Importantly, UN Data is committed to making information publicly accessible supported by Google's Data Commons – removing issues of the legal ownership of data and enhancing accessibility.

9.2.3 Reporting

In addition to the formal progress reports of the HLPF, the UN produces an annual *Sustainable Development Report* which includes details of global progress as well as regional and subnational reports.[19] Infographics, fact sheets and other simplified data are provided on the UN SDG website.[20] Reporting at the national level is less comprehensive, although nations can voluntarily submit a national report to the HLPF for consideration at its meetings, and synthesis reports are prepared.[21]

The 2024 *Sustainable Development Report* is sobering, as it notes that only 16 per cent of the SDG targets are on track, with the remainder either regressing or showing limited progress. Most worrying is the stagnation since 2020, particularly in relation to hunger, cities and communities, life on land

13 Sustainable Development Report, *Methods Summary and Data Tables*, https://dashboards.sdgindex.org/chapters/methodology.

14 UN SDGs, *Cape Town Global Action Plan for Sustainable Development Data*, https://unstats.un.org/sdgs/hlg/cape-town-global-action-plan/.

15 UN SDGs, *Global Database*, https://unstats.un.org/UNSDWebsite/undatacommons/.

16 *UN SDGs, SDG Indicators, https://unstats.un.org/sdgs/metadata/.*

17 UN, *Data Commons for the SDGs*, https://unstats.un.org/UNSDWebsite/undatacommons/sdgs.

18 UN Data, https://unstats.un.org/UNSDWebsite/undatacommons/.

19 UN, *Sustainable Development Goal Report 2024*. The website also includes rankings and scores, interactive maps and country profiles.

20 UN SDGs, *SDGs – Explainers*, https://www.un.org/sustainabledevelopment/sdg-fast-facts/.

21 UN HLPF, *Voluntary National Reviews*, https://hlpf.un.org/vnrs.

and in the oceans, and peace, justice and institutions.[22] SDGs related to food and land systems were found to be particularly off track.[23] Progress that has been made is unevenly spread across the world, with the Nordic countries at the top of the SDG index and Brazil, Russia, India, China and South Africa (BRICS countries) lagging behind.[24] Global cooperation is again highlighted as critical to the achievement of the SDGs, and national commitments vary, with the US ranking last in terms of support for multilateralism. Financing is a key concern, with one key finding being that global financial architecture requires urgent reform.[25] Improving that architecture will require law, policy and governance expertise, as well as business, commerce, finance, investment and economic skills and knowledge.

9.3 Towards 2030

In the 2023 HLPF, *Political Declaration* was adopted, noting that the 'achievement of the SDGs is in peril . . . we are alarmed that the progress on most of the SDGs is either moving much too slowly or has regressed below the 2015 baseline . . . years of sustainable development gains are being reversed'.[26] The member states reaffirmed their commitment to *Agenda 2030* as the 'overarching roadmap for achievement sustainable development' (para 2) before committing to 'bold, ambitious, accelerated, just and transformative actions, anchored in international solidarity and effective cooperation at all levels' (para 9). But how can this rhetoric be turned into a reality? The *Political Declaration* recognises the need for 'a systemic shift towards a more inclusive, just, peaceful, resilient and sustainable world for people and planet, for present and future generations' (para 9). Yet the way in which this shift is to be achieved is unclear, with member states simply pledging to 'taking continuous, fundamental, transformative and urgent actions at all levels and by all stakeholders to overcome the crises and obstacles facing our world' (para 36). As the key body tasked with supporting implementation, it is the HLPF that must identify ways forward in this area.

9.3.1 Realising ambitious acceleration

Overall, the *Political Declaration* emphasises key elements of cooperation (e.g., paras 10, 12 and 17), and effective implementation is highlighted

22 UN, *Sustainable Development Goal Report 2024*, Executive Summary.
23 UN, *Sustainable Development Goal Report 2024.*
24 UN, *Sustainable Development Goal Report 2024.*
25 UN, *Sustainable Development Goal Report 2024.*
26 UNGA, *Political Declaration of the High-Level Political Forum on Sustainable Development Convened Under the Auspices of the General Assembly* (2023), para 8.

(e.g., paras 22, 33), as well as sustainable financing (e.g., paras 30–31). Exploring the *Declaration* through a legal lens, the rule of law and good governance are specifically mentioned as a foundation for 'peaceful, just and inclusive societies' (para 20). Expanding upon the overarching commitments to accelerating action, particular reference was made to 'enhancing and supporting policies and strategies for reducing poverty and inequality' and 'action to remove all legal . . . barriers to achieving gender equality . . . and call for women's full access to justice and effective legal remedies' (para 38). The same paragraph also highlights the importance of integrating the SDGs into national policy frameworks and ensuring policy coherence, as well as increasing 'the use of science and scientific evidence in policymaking' (para 38). This draws attention to the importance of other disciplines, including social, natural and technological sciences. Specific reference is made to the implementation of the *Convention on Biological Diversity*, *UN Framework Convention on Climate Change*, the *Paris Agreement*, the *UN Convention to Combat Desertification*, the *UN Convention on the Law of the Sea* and the *UN Convention Against Corruption* and the *UN Convention Against Transnational Organized Crime*, as well as the development of the new legally binding instrument on plastic pollution (para 38). Again, these international law instruments require a multitude of knowledge and expertise across different fields in order to be effective.

9.3.2 Enhancing cooperation and implementation

Collaboration is at the heart of the SDGs and is needed at all levels and scales, both vertical and horizontal. At the global level, states act through the UN in implementing new international law, development agenda and financing arrangements, for example. Similarly, at the domestic level, cooperation between sub-national levels of government is needed to ensure cohesive approaches to sustainable development. As earlier in this chapter, integration of sustainable development and the SDGs into policies and laws is a recognised area for improvement. Simultaneously, all actors must facilitate participation. Government policies must be inclusive and encourage and support the involvement of all groups of stakeholders. At the same time actors must work together (supported by those policies) to implement their SDG commitments.

From a particular legal perspective, some progress can be seen in implementation at the global level, for example, with the 2022 WTO Agreement on Fisheries Subsidies, whereby governments came together to adopt an international instrument.[27] Yet there are other SDG targets where similar action could

27 WTO, *Agreement on Fisheries Subsidies*, https://www.wto.org/english/tratop_e/rulesneg_e/fish_e/fish_e.htm.

be taken. the HLPF could place some emphasis on law as a tool to achieve the SDGs, perhaps through one of the future annual meetings. In addition, building technical capacity and sharing ideas and examples about law and policy interventions is a useful way in which the UN could support the achievement of those targets that rely upon law and policy instruments. As set out in Chapters 2–8, some targets and indicators refer to specific legal instruments, and others explicitly call for the implementation of law and policy at the national level. Other UN agencies have sought to assist states by providing databases of national laws[28] and country strategies.[29] Sharing resources can provide examples for other nations seeking to enhance implementation through law and policy. Relevantly, to date it has been an NGO that has provided detailed legal guides for each SDG.[30]

9.4 Over the horizon

Beyond the current planned activities, there is a need to look further ahead. Whether or not the SDG targets are met by 2030, the essence of them remains vital if sustainable futures are to be secured for all people and the planet. Just as the SDGs evolved from the MDGs, so too might future goals. The *Political Declaration* recognised the need for systemic shifts, and one of the most critical is changing patterns of consumption and production. This aim has not yet been achieved in any country, and future iterations of the SDGs could embed sustainable consumption and production across all goals with quantified percentages and time limits throughout. Potentially there is a greater role for non-state actors such as corporations. The private sector has continued to grow in influence, and this trend is likely to continue. As critical global actors, corporations might hold the key to sustainable production. Simultaneously, changes in consumption require new ideas and approaches, and inclusivity of all peoples in identifying them is vital. In particular, it is younger generations that will bear the future consequences of unsustainable activities now, and so the greater involvement of youth may be crucial.

28 See, for example, UNESCO, *Database of National Cultural Heritage Laws*, https://www.unesco.org/en/articles/unesco-database-national-cultural-heritage-laws-updated and the UNOOSA National Space Laws, https://www.unoosa.org/oosa/en/ourwork/spacelaw/nationalspacelaw/index.html.

29 See, for example, CBD, *National Biodiversity Strategies and Action Plans*, https://www.cbd.int/nbsap.

30 Advocates for International Development, *SDG Legal Initiative*, https://www.a4id.org/a-legal-guide-to-the-sustainable-development-goals/.

9.5 Concluding comments

The global community is more than halfway through the 15-year journey to achieve the SDGs and yet we are 'severely off track'.[31] The HLPF has noted that '[w]ithout immediate course correction and acceleration of progress toward achieving the SDGs, our world is destined to face continued poverty, prolonged periods of crisis and growing uncertainty'.[32] Given the stagnation and regression in recent years, there are no doubt opportunities to bolster support for international law instruments and institutions aligned with the SDGs and to better utilise law and policy at the national level to achieve the SDGs. The achievement of the goals, though, will involve all disciplines and all stakeholders if meaningful changes are to be brought about to alter our trajectory.

31 *The Sustainable Development Goals Report 2024*, 4.
32 UNGA, *Political Declaration of the High-Level Political Forum . . .*, para 24.

Bibliography

Abidjan Principles on the Right to Education (2019), https://www.abidjan-principles.org/.

Advocates for International Development, *SDG 16: Peace, Justice and Strong Institutions – A Legal Guide* (London: A4ID, 2021).

Advocates for International Development, *SDG 4: Quality Education – A Legal Guide* (London: A4ID, 2022a).

Advocates for International Development, *SDG 6: Clean Water and Sanitation* (London: A4ID, 2022b).

Advocates for International Development, *SDG 1: No Poverty – A Legal Guide* (London: A4ID, 2023a).

Advocates for International Development, *SDG 14: Life Below Water – A Legal Guide* (London: A4ID, 2023b).

Advocates for International Development, *SDG 17: Partnerships for the Goals – A Legal Guide* (London: A4ID, 2023c).

Advocates for International Development, *SDG 7: Affordable and Clean Energy – A Legal Guide* (London: A4ID, 2024a).

Advocates for International Development, *SDG 8: Decent Work and Economic Growth – A Legal Guide* (London: A4ID, 2024b).

Advocates for International Development, *SDG 9: Industry, Innovation and Infrastructure – A Legal Guide* (London: A4ID, 2024c).

Advocates for International Development, *SDG 10: Reduced inequality – A Legal Guide* (London: A4ID, 2024d).

Advocates for International Development, *SDG Legal Initiative*, https://www.a4id.org/a-legal-guide-to-the-sustainable-development-goals/.

Agenda 21 (1992), https://www.un.org/en/conferences/environment/rio1992.

Agreement Between the Government of Hungary and the Government of the Republic of Cabo Verde for the Promotion and Reciprocal Protection of Investments (Cape Verde, Hungary: BIT, 2019), https://edit.wti.org/document/show/46bdb04e-721b-4cac-830a-1c346c25c96c.

Arcuri, Alessandra and Enrico Partiti, 'SDG 12: Ensure Sustainable Consumption and Production Patterns' in J Ebbesson and E Hey (eds), *The Cambridge Handbook of The Sustainable Development Goals and International Law* (Cambridge: CUP, 2022) 304.

Australia's Select Committees on Air Pollution and Water Pollution 1968–70, http://navigatesenatecommittees.senate.gov.au/events/select-committees-on-air-pollution-and-water-pollution/62.

Bantekas, Ilias and Katerina Akestoridi, 'Sustainable Development Goals, between Politics and Soft Law: The Emergence of "Political Normativity" in International Law' (2023) 37 *Emory International Law Review* 499.

Basel Convention, https://www.basel.int/.

Birkenkötter, Hannah, 'SDG 12: Ensure Sustainable Consumption and Production Patterns' in Ilias Bantekas and Francesco Seatzu (eds), *The UN Sustainable Development Goals: A Commentary* (Oxford: OUP, 2024).

Bodansky, Daniel, 'SDG13: Take Urgent Action to Combat Climate Change and Its Impacts' in J Ebbesson and E Hey (eds), *The Cambridge Handbook of The Sustainable Development Goals and International Law* (Cambridge: CUP, 2022).

Bruce, Stuart and Jorge E Viñuales, 'SDG7: Ensure Access to Affordable, Reliable, Sustainable and Modern Energy for All' in J Ebbesson and E Hey (eds), *The Cambridge Handbook of The Sustainable Development Goals and International Law* (Cambridge: CUP, 2022).

CBD, *Aichi Biodiversity Targets*, https://www.cbd.int/sp/targets.

CBD, *The Biodiversity Plan*, https://www.cbd.int/gbf.

CBD, *The Nagoya Protocol on Access and Benefit-Sharing*, https://www.cbd.int/abs/default.shtml.

CBD, *National Biodiversity Strategies and Action Plans*, https://www.cbd.int/nbsap.

Convention on Biological Diversity, www.cbd.int.

Coomans, Fons, 'SDG 4: Ensure Inclusive and Equitable Quality Education and Promote Lifelong Learning Opportunities for All' in J Ebbesson and E Hey (eds), *The Cambridge Handbook of The Sustainable Development Goals and International Law* (Cambridge: CUP, 2022).

Copenhagen Declaration on Social Development (UNGA/Conf.166/9, March 14, 1995), https://www.un.org/en/development/desa/population/migration/generalassembly/docs/globalcompact/A_CONF.166_9_Declaration.pdf.

Cullet, Philippe, 'SDG 10: Reduce Inequality Within and Among Countries' in J Ebbesson and E Hey (eds), *The Cambridge Handbook of The Sustainable Development Goals and International Law* (Cambridge: CUP, 2022).

Dhahri S and A Omri, 'Are International Capital Flows Really Matter for Achieving SDGs 1 and 2: Ending Poverty and Hunger?' (2020) 156 *Review of World Economics* 731–767.

du Plessis, Anél, 'SDG 11: Make Cities and Human Settlements Inclusive, Safe, Resilient and Sustainable' in J Ebbesson and E Hey (eds), *The Cambridge Handbook of The Sustainable Development Goals and International Law* (Cambridge: CUP, 2022).

Duvic-Paoli, Leslie-Anne, 'From Aspirational Politics to Soft Law? Exploring the International Legal Effects of Sustainable Development Goal 7 on Affordable and Clean Energy' (2021) 22(1) *Melbourne Journal of International Law* 1–23.

Ebbesson, J and E Hey, 'Introduction: The Sustainable Development Goals, Agenda 2030 and International Law' in J Ebbesson and E Hey (eds), *The Cambridge Handbook of The Sustainable Development Goals and International Law* (Cambridge: CUP, 2022).

EIF, https://www.enhancedif.org/.

Elliott, Lorraine, 'History of the Environmental Movement' (*Brittanica*, October 11, 2024), https://www.britannica.com/topic/environmentalism/History-of-the-environmental-movement.

Environment America, *From Earth Day 1970 to 2022: A Story of Progress*, https://environmentamerica.org/center/articles/earth-day-1970-2022-story-progress/.

FAO, 'FAO Report: Global Fisheries and Aquaculture Production Reaches a New Record High' (*FAO Newsroom*, June 7, 2024), https://www.fao.org/newsroom/detail/fao-report-global-fisheries-and-aquaculture-production-reaches-a-new-record-high/en.

FAO, IFAD and WFP, *The State of Food Insecurity in the World 2014* (Rome: FAO, 2014).

Food and Agriculture Organization, *About FAO*, https://www.fao.org/about/about-fao/en/.

Fourie, Andria Naudé, 'SDG 9: Build Resilient Infrastructure, Promote Inclusive and Sustainable Industrialization and Foster Innovation' in J Ebbesson and E Hey (eds), *The Cambridge Handbook of The Sustainable Development Goals and International Law* (Cambridge: CUP, 2022).

Gasper, Des, Amod Shar and Sunil Tankha, 'The Framing of Sustainable Consumption and Production in SDG 12' (2019) 10(1) *Global Policy* 83.

Gonzalez, Carmen, 'SDG2: End Hunger, Achieve Food Security and Improved Nutrition and Promote Sustainable Agriculture' in J Ebbesson and E Hey (eds), *The Cambridge Handbook of The Sustainable Development Goals and International Law* (Cambridge: CUP, 2022).

Green Climate Fund, https://www.greenclimate.fund/.

Guiry, Niamh, 'International Law & the Sustainable Development Goals' (2024) 7 *The Boolean* 1.

Gupta, Joyeeta and Hilmer Bosch, 'SDG 6: Clean Water and Sanitation' in J Ebbesson and E Hey (eds), *The Cambridge Handbook of The Sustainable Development Goals and International Law* (Cambridge: CUP, 2022).

ILO Declaration of Philadelphia (1944), https://webapps.ilo.org/static/english/inwork/cb-policy-guide/declarationofPhiladelphia1944.pdf.

IMF, *Support for Low-Income Countries*, https://www.imf.org/en/About/Factsheets/IMF-Support-for-Low-Income-Countries.

International Council for Science, *A Guide to SDG Interactions: From Science to Implementation* (2017), https://council.science/wp-content/uploads/2017/05/SDGs-Guide-to-Interactions.pdf.

IUCN Red List, https://www.iucnredlist.org/.

Kameri-Mbote, Patricia and Nkatha Kabira, 'SDG 5: Achieve Gender Equality and Empower All Women and Girls' in J Ebbesson and E Hey (eds), *The Cambridge Handbook of The Sustainable Development Goals and International Law* (Cambridge: CUP, 2022).

Kruk, Margaret E et al, 'Mortality Due to Low-Quality Health Systems in the Universal Health Coverage Era: A Systematic Analysis of Amenable Deaths in 137 Countries' (2018) 392(10160) *The Lancet* 2203–2212.
Marine Protection Atlas, https://mpatlas.org/.
McCauley, D et al., 'Marine Defaunation: Animal Loss in the Global Ocean' (2015) 347(6219) *Science* 1255641.
Millennium Declaration (2000), https://documents.un.org/doc/undoc/gen/n00/559/51/pdf/n0055951.pdf.
Millennium Development Goals and Beyond (2015), https://www.un.org/millenniumgoals/.
Mitkidis, Kateřina and Adriana Šefčíková, 'SDG12: Ensure Sustainable Consumption and Productions Patterns' in Ilias Bantekas and Francesco Seatzu (eds), *The UN Sustainable Development Goals: A Commentary* (Oxford: OUP, 2024).
Morgera, Elisa, 'SDG15: Protect, Restore and Promote Sustainable Use of Terrestrial Ecosystems, Sustainably Manage Forests, Combat Desertification, and Halt and Reverse Land Degradation and Halt Biodiversity Loss' in J Ebbesson and E Hey (eds), *The Cambridge Handbook of the Sustainable Development Goals and International Law* (Cambridge: CUP, 2022).
National Geographic, 'Anthropocene', https://education.nationalgeographic.org/resource/anthropocene/.
Novitz, Tonia, 'SDG 8: Promote Sustained, Inclusive and Sustainable Economic Growth, Full and Productive Employment and Decent Work for All' in J Ebbesson and E Hey (eds), *The Cambridge Handbook of the Sustainable Development Goals and International Law* (Cambridge: CUP, 2022).
OECD, *Guidelines for Multinational Enterprises on Responsible Business Conduct* (Paris: OECD Publishing, 2023).
Our World in Data, *Mountain Green Cover Index*, https://ourworldindata.org/grapher/mountain-green-cover-index.
Our World in Data, *SDG Tracker: Measuring Progress Towards the Sustainable Development Goals*, https://ourworldindata.org/sdgs.
Our World in Data, *Urbanization*, https://ourworldindata.org/urbanization.
Ploska, A, 'All Beginnings Are Difficult: The Guiding Principles on Extreme Poverty and Human Rights a Decade After Their Adoption' (2023) 23(2) *Human Rights Law Review* 1–21.
Rachovitsa, Adamantia and Marlies Hesselman, 'Introduction to the Special Issue: International Law for the Sustainable Development Goals' (2019) 2 *Brill Open Law* 1–7.
Rotterdam Convention, https://www.pic.int/.
Scott, Karen, 'SDG 14. Conserve and Sustainably Use the Oceans, Seas and Marine Resources for Sustainable Development' in J Ebbsson and E Hey (eds), *The Cambridge Handbook of the Sustainable Development Goals and International Law* (Cambridge: Cambridge University Press, 2022).
Spijkers, Otto, 'Sustainable Management of Freshwater Resources: Linking International Water Law and the Sustainable Development Goals' (2019) 28(2) *GAIA – Ecological Perspectives for Science and Society* 135–142.
Stockholm Convention, https://chm.pops.int/.

Stockholm Resilience Centre, Planetary boundaries, https://www.stockholmresilience.org/research/planetary-boundaries.html

Sustainable Development Report, *Methods Summary and Data Tables*, https://dashboards.sdgindex.org/chapters/methodology.

Techera, Erika and Joy McCann, *The Unruly Ocean: Law and Justice in the World's Oceans Seas and Shorelines* (Abingdon: Routledge, 2025).

Tladi, Dire, 'SDG1: End Poverty in All Its Forms Everywhere' in J Ebbesson and E Hey (eds), *The Cambridge Handbook of The Sustainable Development Goals and International Law* (Cambridge: Cambridge University Press, 2022).

TRAFFIC, https://www.traffic.org/.

UN, *Charter of the United Nations* (1945), https://www.un.org/en/about-us/un-charter.

UN, *Climate Action*, https://www.un.org/en/climatechange/net-zero-coalition.

UN, *Conference on Environment and Sustainable Development (Rio Conference)*, https://www.un.org/en/conferences/environment.

UN, *Conference on Sustainable Development*, https://www.un.org/en/conferences/environment/rio2012.

UN, *Conference on the Human Environment*, https://www.un.org/en/conferences/environment/stockholm1972.

UN, *Conferences – Habitat*, https://www.un.org/en/conferences/habitat.

UN, *Country Classification*, https://www.un.org/en/development/desa/policy/wesp/wesp_current/2014wesp_country_classification.pdf.

UN, *Data Commons for the SDGs*, https://unstats.un.org/UNSDWebsite/undatacommons/sdgs.

UN, *Department of Economic and Social Affairs, Sustainable Development*, https://sdgs.un.org/goals.

UN, *Division for Ocean Affairs and the Law of the Sea*, https://www.un.org/depts/los/convention_agreements/convention_overview_convention.htm.

UN, *Educate Girls, Eradicate Poverty – A Mutually Reinforcing Goal*, https://www.un.org/en/chronicle/article/educate-girls-eradicate-poverty-mutually-reinforcing-goal.

UN, *High-Level Political Forum*, https://hlpf.un.org/.

UN, *The Millennium Development Goals Report 2015* (2015), https://www.un.org/millenniumgoals/2015_MDG_Report/pdf/MDG%202015%20rev%20(July%201).pdf.

UN, *Millennium Summit*, https://www.un.org/en/conferences/environment/newyork2000.

UN, *SDG Indicators*, https://unstats.un.org/sdgs/indicators/indicators-list/.

UN, *Sustainable Development Goals*, https://www.un.org/sustainabledevelopment/.

UN, *The Sustainable Development Goals Report 2024*, https://dashboards.sdgindex.org/.

UN, *United Nations Conference on the Human Environment*, https://www.un.org/en/conferences/environment/stockholm1972.

UN, *Universal Declaration of Human Rights*, https://www.un.org/en/about-us/universal-declaration-of-human-rights.

UN Climate Change, 'What is the Triple Planetary Crisis?' (*UNFCCC Blog*, April 13, 2022), https://unfccc.int/news/what-is-the-triple-planetary-crisis.

UN Climate Change, www.unfccc.int.

UN Climate Change, *What is the Kyoto Protocol?* https://unfccc.int/kyoto_protocol.

UN Climate Change, *What is the Paris Agreement?* https://unfccc.int/process-and-meetings/the-paris-agreement.

UN Data, https://unstats.un.org/UNSDWebsite/undatacommons/.

UN Declaration on the Right to Development (1986), https://www.ohchr.org/en/instruments-mechanisms/instruments/declaration-right-development.

UN General Assembly, *Report of the United Nations Conference on the Human Environment* (A/Conf.48/14/Rev.1, 1972), https://documents.un.org/doc/undoc/gen/nl7/300/05/pdf/nl730005.pdf.

UN General Assembly, *Declaration on the Right to Development* (UNGA Res 41/128, December 4, 1986), https://www.ohchr.org/en/instruments-mechanisms/instruments/declaration-right-development.

UN General Assembly, *Report of the World Commission on Environment and Development, Our Common Future* (UNGA Res 42/427, annex, August 4, 1987), https://sustainabledevelopment.un.org/content/documents/5987our-common-future.pdf.

UN General Assembly, *The Future We Want. Outcome document of the UN Conference on Sustainable Development* (A/Res 66/288, 2012), https://sustainabledevelopment.un.org/index.php?menu=1298.

UN General Assembly, *Transforming Our World: The 2030 Agenda for Sustainable Development* (A/RES/70/1, 2015), https://sdgs.un.org/2030agenda.

UN General Assembly, *Global Indicator Framework for the Sustainable Development Goals and Targets of the 2030 Agenda for Sustainable Development* (A/Res 71/313, 2017a), https://unstats.un.org/sdgs/indicators/Global-Indicator-Framework-after-2024-refinement-English.pdf.

UN General Assembly, *Work of the Statistical Commission Pertaining to the 2030 Agenda for Sustainable Development* (A/RES/71/313, July 10, 2017b), https://documents.un.org/doc/undoc/gen/n17/207/63/pdf/n1720763.pdf.

UN General Assembly, *The Right to Food in the Context of International Trade Law and Policy, Interim Report of the Special Rapporteur on the Right to Food* (A/75/219, July 22, 2020), https://digitallibrary.un.org/record/3879225?ln=en&v=pdf.

UN General Assembly, *Political Declaration of the High-Level Political Forum on Sustainable Development Convened Under the Auspices of the General Assembly* (UNGA Res 78/1, October 16, 2023), https://www.un.org/en/conferences/SDGSummit2023/political-declaration.

UN General Assembly, *Progress Towards the Sustainable Development Goals* (UNGA Res A/79/79, May 2, 2024), https://unstats.un.org/sdgs/files/report/2024/SG-SDG-Progress-Report-2024-advanced-unedited-version.pdf.

UN Habitat, https://unhabitat.org/.

UN Habitat, *The New Urban Agenda*, https://habitat3.org/the-new-urban-agenda/.

UN HLPF, *Mandate and Functions*, https://hlpf.un.org/mandate-and-functions.

UN HLPF, *Voluntary National Reviews*, https://hlpf.un.org/vnrs.

UN Human Rights Office of the High Commissioner, *Special Rapporteur on Extreme Poverty and Human Rights*, https://www.ohchr.org/en/special-procedures/sr-poverty.
UN Human Rights Office of the High Commissioner, *Special Rapporteur on the Right to Education*, https://www.ohchr.org/en/special-procedures/sr-education.
UN Human Rights Office of the High Commissioner, *Working Group on the Right to Development*, https://www.ohchr.org/en/hrc-subsidiaries/iwg-on-development.
UN SDGs, https://sdgs.un.org/.
UN SDGs, *Actions Platform*, https://sdgs.un.org/partnerships.
UN SDGs, *Cape Town Global Action Plan for Sustainable Development Data*, https://unstats.un.org/sdgs/hlg/cape-town-global-action-plan/.
UN SDGs, *Global Database, UN Data*, https://unstats.un.org/UNSDWebsite/undatacommons/.
UN SDGs, *Goal 5: Achieve Gender Equality and Empower All Women and Girls*, https://www.un.org/sustainabledevelopment/gender-equality/.
UN SDGs, *Goal 11: Make Cities Inclusive, Safe, Resilient and Sustainable*, https://www.un.org/sustainabledevelopment/cities/.
UN SDGs, *Goal 16: Promote Just, Peaceful and Inclusive Societies,* https://www.un.org/sustainabledevelopment/peace-justice/.
UN SDGs, *Goal 17: Revitalize the Global Partnership for Sustainable Development,* https://www.un.org/sustainabledevelopment/globalpartnerships/.
UN SDGs, *SDG Indicators*, https://unstats.un.org/sdgs/metadata/.
UN SDGs, *SDGs – Explainers*, https://www.un.org/sustainabledevelopment/sdg-fast-facts/.
UN Water, *Human Rights to Water and Sanitation*, www.unwater.org/water-facts/human-rights-water-and-sanitation.
UNCTAD, *Food Export Restrictions Hurt Millions in Least Developed Countries,* https://unctad.org/topic/least-developed-countries/chart-march-to-june-2022.
UNCTAD, *Key Statistics on LDCs*, https://unctad.org/topic/least-developed-countries/chart-of-the-month.
UNDESA, *UN 10-Year Framework of Programmes on Sustainable Consumption and Production Patterns* (2014), https://sdgs.un.org/publications/10-year-framework-programmes-sustainable-consumption-and-production-patterns-10yfp.
UNDP, *Having a Legal Identity is Fundamental to Human Rights*, https://www.undp.org/africa/blog/having-legal-identity-fundamental-human-rights.
UNDRR, *Sendai Framework on Disaster Risk Reduction 2015–2030*, https://www.undrr.org/publication/sendai-framework-disaster-risk-reduction-2015-2030.
UNEP, *About Montreal Protocol*, https://www.unep.org/ozonaction/who-we-are/about-montreal-protocol.
UNEP, *Intergovernmental Negotiating Committee (INC) on Plastic Pollution*, https://www.unep.org/inc-plastic-pollution.
UNEP, *Ozone Treaties*, https://ozone.unep.org/.
UNEP, *Species+*, https://www.speciesplus.net/.
UNEP, *WCMC*, https://www.unep-wcmc.org/en.

UNESCO, *Database of National Cultural Heritage Laws*, https://www.unesco.org/en/articles/unesco-database-national-cultural-heritage-laws-updated.

UNESCO, *Marine Policy*, https://www.ioc.unesco.org/en/marine-policy.

UNESCO, *Ocean Plastic Pollution an Overview: Data and Statistics*, https://oceanliteracy.unesco.org/plastic-pollution-ocean/.

UNESCO, *Sustainable Cities*, https://www.unesco.org/en/sustainable-cities.

UNESCO, *World Heritage Convention*, https://whc.unesco.org/en/convention/.

UNOOSA National Space Laws, https://www.unoosa.org/oosa/en/ourwork/spacelaw/nationalspacelaw/index.html.

WHO, *Constitution of the World Health Organization* (1946), https://apps.who.int/gb/bd/PDF/bd47/EN/constitution-en.pdf?ua=1.

WHO, *Global Targets 2025: To Improve Maternal, Infant and Young Child Nutrition*, https://www.who.int/teams/nutrition-and-food-safety/global-targets-2025.

WIPO, *Global Innovation Index*, https://www.wipo.int/web/global-innovation-index.

World Bank Group, *Building Sustainable Cities & Communities*, https://www.worldbank.org/en/topic/sustainable-communities.

World Bank Group, *Ending Poverty and Ensuring Dignity for All*, https://www.worldbank.org/en/news/feature/2023/10/16/end-poverty-and-ensure-dignity-for-all.

Wrange, Pål, 'SDG 16: Promote Peaceful and Inclusive Societies for Sustainable Development, Provide Access to Justice for All and Build Effective, Accountable and Inclusive Institutions at All Levels' in J Ebbesson and E Hey (eds), *The Cambridge Handbook of The Sustainable Development Goals and International Law* (Cambridge: CUP, 2022).

WTO, *Agreement on Fisheries Subsidies*, https://www.wto.org/english/tratop_e/rulesneg_e/fish_e/fish_e.htm.

WTO, *The Doha Round*, https://www.wto.org/english/tratop_e/dda_e/dda_e.htm.

WTO, *Legal Texts*, https://www.wto.org/english/docs_e/legal_e/legal_e.htm.

WTO, *Marrakesh Agreement Establishing the World Trade Organization*, https://www.wto.org/english/docs_e/legal_e/04-wto_e.htm.

WTO, *Overview: the TRIPS Agreement*, https://www.wto.org/english/tratop_e/trips_e/intel2_e.htm.

WTO, *Principles of the Trading System,* https://www.wto.org/english/thewto_e/whatis_e/tif_e/fact2_e.htm.

WTO, *Special and Differential Treatment Provisions*, https://www.wto.org/english/tratop_e/devel_e/dev_special_differential_provisions_e.htm.

WTO, *What We Stand For*, https://www.wto.org/english/thewto_e/whatis_e/what_stand_for_e.htm.

WTO, *The WTO and the Sustainable Development Goals,* https://www.wto.org/english/thewto_e/coher_e/sdgs_e/sdgs_e.htm.

Index

FSC
www.fsc.org
MIX
Papier | Fördert gute Waldnutzung
FSC® C083411

Kolibri 360 GmbH
Ferdinand-Jühlke-Straße 7
99095 Erfurt, Deutschland
produktsicherheit@kolibri360.de